CITY BY DESIGN

an architectural perspective of texas

Published by

PANACHE
P A N A C H E   P A R T N E R S

Panache Partners, LLC
1424 Gables Court
Plano, Texas 75075
469.246.6060
Fax: 469.246.6062
www.panache.com

Publishers: Brian G. Carabet and John A. Shand

Printed in Malaysia

Distributed by IPG
800.748.5439

PUBLISHER'S DATA

City by Design Texas

Library of Congress Control Number: 2008920703

ISBN 13:   978-1-933415-56-7
ISBN 10:   1-933415-56-8

First Printing 2008

10 9 8 7 6 5 4 3 2 1

PREVIOUS PAGE: Texas Association of Counties, Steinbomer & Associates Architecture, *page 182*
Photograph by Osborne Photography

RIGHT: United Way of the Texas Gulf Coast, Gensler, *page 224*
Photograph by Joe Aker, Aker/Zvonkovic Photography

Panache Partners, LLC, is dedicated to the restoration and conservation of the environment.
Our *City by Design* books are manufactured with strict adherence to an environmental
management system in accordance with ISO 14001 standards, including the use of paper
from mills certified to derive their products from environmentally managed forests. We are
committed to continued investigation of alternative paper products and environmentally
responsible manufacturing processes to ensure the preservation of our fragile planet.

CITY BY DESIGN

an architectural perspective of texas

FOREWORD

In a state as varied and multicultural as Texas, it is to be expected that its built environment is truly an aesthetically heterogeneous structural tapestry. To be certain, any chronicle of the remarkable array of architectural achievements across such a grand state must first be rooted in comprehension of Texas' extraordinarily diverse composition.

Spanning 790 miles long and 660 miles wide at its farthest points, the Lone Star State is larger than New England, New York, Ohio, Pennsylvania and North Carolina combined. Its prodigious reach and immense scale are only surpassed by its eclectic geographic grandeur: east Texas is thick with mature pine forests; lowland marshes and bayous characterize the Texas coastal bend; bordering Mexico, the Rio Grande Valley, actually a river delta, features fertile floodplains long used for ranching; great plains and prairies comprise much of central and north Texas; the Hill Country, a portion of the Edwards Plateau in central Texas, includes a wondrous array of rugged, rolling hills; to the west, El Paso, closer to California than Dallas, is home to an arid region of desert valleys, wooded mountain slopes and desert grasslands, with multiple peaks eclipsing 8,000 feet.

This incomparable terrain serves as a transcendent canvas through which creative and skilled architects erect distinguished structures—from sleek, modern skyscrapers in Dallas and Houston to stately, historic courthouses and museums in Fort Worth, from naturalistic, stone structures inspired by the Hill Country's innate beauty to old Victorian neighborhoods redolent of San Francisco found in Galveston, the aesthetic quality of Texas' architectural fabric is truly unique.

This variety of geographic palettes is just one of many factors affecting Texas' built surroundings, according to Larry Speck, FAIA, principal of PageSoutherlandPage and former dean of the University of Texas School of Architecture. "Texas architectural design is shaped by the uniqueness of the region itself—the striking and extremely varied geography, the hot and sunny climate, the richness of building materials and the warm, open populous the state has attracted," Larry says. "All of these elements become form-determinates in the best of Texas architecture."

Already a resplendent repository of architectural prowess, Dallas will soon be the only city to boast structures designed by four different Pritzker Prize-winning architects: I.M. Pei's Morton H. Meyerson Symphony Center, Renzo Piano's Nasher Sculpture Center, Sir Norman Foster's Margot and Bill Winspear Opera House and Rem Koolhaas' Dee and Charles Wyly Theatre. Well known for its striking mid-century modern architecture, Dallas has committed to rejuvenating its urban core, says AIA Dallas Executive Director Paula Clements. "There has been a lot of emphasis placed on redevelopment and bringing people back to the cities," Paula relates, noting the conversion of a brownfield site into the now-bustling Victory Park development.

This emphasis on establishing denser urban cores is in many ways a result of Texans' larger emphasis on growing in a responsible manner predicated on sustainable design and building. "The banal sameness of American suburban and 'loopland' environments that dominated new building in Texas in the late 20th century is being replaced by downtowns, neighborhoods and parks that have some really authentic character and appeal," Larry says. It is these laudable efforts that have already spurned myriad mixed-use developments and ambitious in-city projects that reflect a genuine commitment to conserving our natural environment.

While the relatively new emphasis on sustainability has unleashed a variety of exciting, new, green products, which in turn have procured sleek, progressive buildings of a more modern aesthetic, Texas' longstanding cultural nuances are very much reflected in its architectural texture. "Texas architectural design is special because it is a mix of unique cultures—the influences of Mexican, European and coastal traditions are evidenced throughout different areas of our truly large and great state," says AIA Fort Worth Executive Director Suzie Adams. "We are seeing a mix of Texas vernacular style with contemporary architecture."

With an eye toward the future, the extraordinary architects throughout Texas are guided by the traditions and rich cultural legacies that define the Lone Star State. It is this commitment to the state's vibrant past, present and future that has made its built environment at once engaging, enduring, eclectic and distinctly Texan.

Carl Wunsche Sr. High School, SHW Group - Houston, page 138

INTRODUCTION

Each day we pass by hundreds of buildings—a mélange of old and new works of architecture—that we likely take entirely for granted, not because of a lack of interest but rather because we move at a pace too swift to ask ourselves why, how, when and through whose creativity did the architecture come to fruition. Yet it is these very structures, unassuming or prominently placed, that create the brilliantly complex urban and suburban landscapes where our lives unfold.

Imagine being afforded the rare opportunity to gaze inside the walls and around the full perimeter of these buildings that are equal parts mysterious, familiar and alluring. Imagine meeting their creators and discovering the forward-thinking design savvy behind the selection of each material, the placement of each door and window, the sculptural use of both classical and contemporary architectural forms. Now turn the page—commence an invigorating journey that is sure to inspire your appreciation or renew your passion for Texas' architectural fabric.

You will immediately discern *City by Design Texas* as unique among architectural collections. Indeed, it boasts vibrant photographs of stimulating designs mingled with insightful editorial, yet it does not endeavor to present merely the tallest, widest, newest, oldest or greenest buildings. More precisely, it is a rich, diverse collection of the state's best—from landmark skyscrapers that define majestic metropolitan skylines to smaller, thoughtfully designed edifices of some of the suburbs' best-kept secrets. It is a regional compilation of masterfully conceived structures considered the best of the best by the locally based architects and developers who have turned intangible ideas into built realities that will be enjoyed for generations to come.

CONTENTS

Aneita Fern

■ ■

Booziotis & Company Architects

■ ■ ■ ■ ■ ■ ■ ■ ■ ■ Born and raised in the Midwest, Aneita Fern held a strong affinity for the finer things in life—family, compelling design, craftsmanship and beautiful collectibles, particularly antiques. This reverence for astute design and generational pieces was passed down through her family, providing the inspiration for her grandson Christopher Walthall and his family to open an extraordinary store in her name offering distinctive furniture, primarily richly crafted, venerable, high-end Stickley furniture, each piece of which endures and will be a sought-after antique in future years. Designed by the Booziotis & Company Architects team, led by Ann Abernathy, Aneita Fern—the exclusive home of fine Stickley and Frank Lloyd Wright furniture in Dallas-Fort Worth—is a veritable furniture museum for a host of eclectic pieces, and an architectural marvel worthy of hosting such fine works of craftsmanship.

FACING PAGE: Dualities of interlocking vertical and horizontal elements, weight and weightlessness, light and shadow enliven the south façade of the flagship Aneita Fern store, located in a retail strip in north Dallas.
Photograph by Charles Davis Smith, AIA

Located in a retail shopping center across the street from the Dallas Galleria, the showroom needed a striking exterior appearance that would catch the eyes of passersby and draw them in. The store's long and linear composition with both north- and south-facing entrances was outfitted with a compelling, modern south façade while the north face took on more of an Arts-and-Crafts vernacular; this decision reflected the wide range of furniture styles featured within, which spans from Arts-and-Crafts to Prairie through mid-century modern and contemporary periods, as well as the desire to create a neutral setting that would enhance all those periods without overpowering the furniture.

Entrance into either end of the narrow, linear space immerses patrons in a particular period, be it modern or Craftsman, and as one moves through the store the period changes slightly. Ceilings were raised in both entries so the entrance area is very open, and the space narrows as it progresses toward the middle's central glade under a luminous, stained glass lay-light, where the vista to the other side inevitably pulls patrons to the other end. A vortex in section and plan, the showroom employs smaller design elements that augment the compression and expansion of space, such as ubiquitous horizontal banding emblematic of

LEFT: The rhythmic progression of columns and undulating levels draws the visitor to the central space, where blue-green light filters through the lay-light. From there the vista beyond beckons to complete the journey in architectural flow.
Photograph by Charles Davis Smith, AIA

FACING PAGE TOP: Furniture vignettes are created only by pools of light, punctuating columns and screens in the open plan. The ledges are effectively the lighting fixtures as indirect light provides general illumination. All accent lights and air diffusers are recessed, creating luminous ceiling edges with dark reveals. The design of the cashier stations, fireplaces, wood screens and store fixtures repeat the faceting and flow of the overall architecture.
Photograph by Charles Davis Smith, AIA

FACING PAGE BOTTOM: Ann Abernathy's abstract design for the central lay-light recalls the splendid use of art glass in Prairie-style architecture, but was locally inspired—it is an impression of light and color derived from kayaking along the Brazos River. Incorporating more than 2,000 pieces of glass, the lay-light was crafted by Foster Stained Glass.
Photograph by Charles Davis Smith, AIA

the designs of Frank Lloyd Wright—who was a great inspiration to the showroom, which also includes Frank Lloyd Wright Foundation-approved furniture and accessories. In addition to incorporating the store's geometry into display elements, hardware, lighting and other features, the showroom is warmed by abundant natural wood, soft uplighting on the ceiling and recessed accent lights; this homey aura also enables patrons to envision how pieces would look in their own residence.

A one-of-a-kind showroom for incredible Stickley furniture and related products, Aneita Fern is much more than just a retail furniture outlet—it has the welcoming serenity of a library or museum, affording an ideal ambience to showcase the rich craftsmanship evidenced in these illustrious furniture collectibles. ■ ■ ■ ■ ■ ■ ■ ■ ■ ■ ■

Bayou Place II

Powers Brown Architecture

■ ■ ■ ■ ■ ■ ■ ■ ■ ■ The 2003 completion of phase II of Houston's Bayou Place concluded the transformation of what had once been the Albert Thomas Convention Center into a burgeoning mixed-use district adjacent to Buffalo Bayou within downtown's bustling theater and central business district. Powers Brown Architecture's renovation of the original phase and subsequent design of phase II has given rise to a distinctive mixed-use center in a hybrid urban district and park setting.

While a previous renovation phase had brought a host of retail and entertainment options to the north side of Bagby Street, which divides the two phases, the second phase called for the existing structure to provide loft office space directly adjacent to the bayou. In the initial planning stages, consideration was given to cutting a portion of the building off, which would have provided an ideal setting for a housing project, but topography issues related to

FACING PAGE: Abutting Buffalo Bayou, Houston's foremost natural asset, Bayou Place's expansive glass exterior takes advantage of the compelling views.
Photograph by Geoffrey Lyon

the bayou's massive flooding from Tropical Storm Allison would have prevented rebuilding on that parcel. Thus, the decision was made to renovate.

Phase II was chosen as loft office space to take advantage of the high and clear column-free space of the convention center. Roll-up garage doors, French balconies and hanging terraces were designed and built to create an essential connection between the offices and the lush bayou environment. Expansive glass was used on the exteriors to further that indoor-outdoor connection.

At the time, Jeffrey Brown was serving as the president of AIA's Houston chapter and the opportunity arose to relocate the chapter office from a rather non-descript location on the fifth floor of a semi-suburban building into the new Bayou Place. The AIA Houston office was combined with The Houston Architectural Foundation office and exhibit space to form an extraordinary 5,000-square-foot architecture center. In addition to providing both organizations a robust and flexible space capable of hosting exhibitions and events, the placement within Houston's thriving theater district—it has more theater seats than any American city other than New York— gives great exposure and increased visibility to what is a veritable cultural institution within a bustling cultural district rife with pedestrian traffic.

LEFT: Bayou Place's pedestrian-friendly setting provides great visibility to its 5,000-square-foot architecture center, which houses offices for AIA Houston and The Houston Architectural Foundation.
Photograph by Geoffrey Lyon

FACING PAGE LEFT: The lobby is warmed by the presence of abundant daylight, wood and stone.
Photograph by Geoffrey Lyon

FACING PAGE RIGHT: The renovation of Bayou Place established a true mix of uses and exemplifies the great urban design potential of a renovation endeavor.
Photograph by Geoffrey Lyon

The building connects to the 6.3-mile Houston tunnel system, which called for safeguards in the event of another massive storm like Tropical Storm Allison. As part of the renovation, a series of flood dams were built and the tunnel was connected back into the system so that the building is literally on a subterranean network. Pedestrians can enter the tunnel system four miles downtown and walk to Bayou Place. The replenished landscaping along Buffalo Bayou is comprised of exceptionally hearty, deep-rooted plants. Now, when a regular storm increases the bayou's water level by the customary 15 to 20 feet and the plants are flooded, they survive and even flourish, which has led to an exceptionally green bayou setting with resplendent vistas. Powers Brown's renovation and design to complete Bayou Place has given Houston a vibrant mixed-use district and is a model of a renovation's urban design potential. ▪ ▪ ▪ ▪ ▪ ▪ ▪ ▪ ▪ ▪

Bengal Coast

■ ■

Techcon Dallas, Inc.

■ ■ ■ ■ ■ ■ ■ ■ ■ The opening of Bengal Coast in uptown Dallas has established an exotic fusion of Southeast Asian flavors, spices and ambience in north Texas in a singular restaurant experience. Designed by Bruce Russo, the architecture sought to bring the culinary excitement found in "the other Asia"—India, Thailand, Malaysia and Indonesia—to discerning local dining enthusiasts in a hybrid form combining sit-down dining and faster, casual dining. Techcon Dallas, a firm specializing in restaurant architecture throughout the United States, took the concept and created an ideal setting evoking the Bay of Bengal region in a clean, contemporary form that is the prototype for this unique dining concept.

FACING PAGE: Atmospheric best describes Bengal Coast's casual dining. The dark, hand-scraped floors add a touch of rustic while the furnishings wrap guests in the modern.
Project Design Team: Bruce Russo, Joe Russo, Laura Fate and Victor Badillo.
Photograph by Scott Hagar

Set on the first floor of the Centrum Building, a Dallas high-rise combining retail, residential and office space, the 4,025-square-foot restaurant's location did not present many exterior design opportunities. However, the conversion of a landscaped exterior area into an atrium created a light and airy space that has quickly become one of the more desirable dining areas within the restaurant. The atrium features a translucent roof array with silk fabrics hanging down; vestiges of regional décor—bamboo placemats and floor coverings, stools hand-carved in India and a potted banana tree—found throughout the restaurant further convey the Eastern theme.

Inside the front entry the use of large timber columns makes a strong initial statement and contrasts well with the abundance of tile and stone featured within. Earth-toned tiles and stone are complemented by gold onyx countertops and tumbled onyx on the bar. Colorful silk and similar fabrics provide a softness against the earthen materials. Entrants are greeted in the entry vestibule by a compelling spice wall featuring 15 transparent display cases filled with spices from around the world such as cumin and mustard seed; many patrons have inquired about obtaining their own spice wall for presentation in their homes.

Completed on a very tight schedule—conceptual designs took place in July and the restaurant opened in December—Bengal Coast has provided Dallas restaurant aficionados with a unique fusion of Southeast Asian cuisine in a setting with warm, inviting colors that feels right out of Bollywood. The design by Techcon Dallas afforded a captivating setting that is often commented on as much or more than the food, helping the initial Bengal Coast restaurant achieve great success and paving the way for future locations. ■ ■ ■ ■ ■ ■ ■ ■ ■ ■

TOP RIGHT: A contemporary blast of flavor and color, culinary essentials such as mustard powder adorn the entrance.
Photograph by Scott Hagar

BOTTOM RIGHT: Atrium dining offers patrons the desired outdoor feel, even in the winter months; during spring and summer the large, retractable glass walls allow the outdoors to come in.
Photograph by Scott Hagar

FACING PAGE LEFT: Day and evening, the atrium provides diners with an indulgent feeling in which they are surrounded by subtle glows of light and wisping fabric.
Photograph by Scott Hagar

FACING PAGE RIGHT: Luxurious countertops define the Bengal Coast bar, which is surrounded by hand-sculpted columns made of rustic wood and accented with onyx sconces and pendants.
Photograph by Scott Hagar

Camp for All

■ ■

Curry Boudreaux Architects

■ ■ ■ ■ ■ ■ ■ ■ ■ ■ Conceived as the ideal summer camp getaway for special needs children in the south Texas area, Camp for All has provided a special community with a long-needed destination for outdoor recreation. Originally conceived by a Houston physician, the vision for Camp for All called for not just an accessible camp setting—but a wholly barrier-free environment. Designed by Curry Boudreaux Architects, Camp for All is the successful realization of a shared vision among a number of collaborative organizations devoted to a commendable, long-term mission.

From the initial project vision an extensive site search commenced for a visually interesting parcel of available land—one that would provide a palpable difference to Houston both climatically and geographically—located within a 100-mile radius of Houston. This two-year search led to the selection of a 206-acre tract of undeveloped ranch land in Washington County featuring two lakes, rolling hills and an assortment of oak, cedar, cypress and pine trees.

FACING PAGE: The rustic yet contemporary chapel at Camp for All is part of a summer camp for special needs children.
Photograph by Geoffrey Lyon

During the search, the design team came to appreciate the local agrarian vernacular of this area west of Brenham, gleaning inspiration from the area's cotton mills, barns, dance halls, ranch houses and small-town Texas streetscapes forged through an additive process over time. This rustic aesthetic was applied to the structures comprising Camp for All in a modern composition, alluding to the architectural heritage without compromising contemporary sensibilities and functional requirements.

During the design of this inclusive camp environment sans barriers, it was unanimous that any grand gestures or references to the camp's mission of service to special needs campers were to be avoided. The desire was to eliminate any overt symbols of accessibility, creating the perception that Camp for All is very much a regular summer camp, eliminating stigma for accessibility-challenged attendees. Throughout the camp, thoughtful site planning allowed for roll-in entries instead of ramps with handrails, and lifts that were necessary were made to be removable.

Vehicular traffic is shielded out toward the perimeter, eliminating any auto presence within the interior of the camp. Once on the premises, campers have the freedom to thoroughly traverse the campground thanks to interconnecting concrete walkways between every building. These pathways extend into the outer reaches of camp in a natural, textured way, enabling everyone the

LEFT: Exposed beams and ductwork provide visual interest in this dining hall interior with views through the stage to the meeting hall beyond.
Photograph by Jud Haggard

FACING PAGE TOP: The meeting hall is warmed by abundant wood and expansive views and features an elegant coffered ceiling.
Photograph by Jud Haggard

FACING PAGE BOTTOM: Interconnecting concrete walkways between every building afford passage throughout camp and even extend into the site's more primitive outer reaches.
Photograph by Jud Haggard

opportunity to travel to the camp's more primitive areas. A remarkable rolling treehouse feature allows campers to enter from a gently sloped sidewalk and ascend into a 30-foot-tall treehouse overlooking a heavily wooded ravine—so all campers, wheelchair-bound or not, can enjoy ravine views from an elevated, wooded perch.

With a carefully planned layout of buildings to define the outdoor spaces, which are really the heart of the camp experience, Camp for All recalls the area's rustic heritage and provides Houston's special needs community with an invaluable destination for rural summer solace. ■ ■ ■ ■ ■ ■ ■ ■ ■ ■

Corpus Christi Convention Center and Multipurpose Arena

■ ■

Gignac Associates

■ ■ ■ ■ ■ ■ ■ ■ ■ ■ The heart of Corpus Christi is, of course, the bay with its enchanting vistas and tranquil ambience. So it would seem natural that the city's convention center, located in close proximity to the water, would respond to the area's foremost natural asset. Prior to 2004, however, that was not the case. Thankfully, Gignac Associates, in collaboration with Arquitectonica and TVS, renovated and expanded the American Bank Convention Center, tying it together architecturally with a new multipurpose arena and existing auditorium while making a grand gesture toward the very essence of Corpus Christi—the water.

In initial planning stages it was decided that the new, 10,500-seat American Bank Center Arena would be located next to the convention center to create synergy and so they could share many utilities, most important of which was the loading dock. A U-shaped facility was created for the loading dock,

FACING PAGE: The asymmetric façade to the convention center and arena emits a subtle glow in the evening.
Project Design Team: Raymond Gignac and Rolando Garza, Gignac Associates; Bernado Fort Brescia, Arquitectonica; Kevin Gordon and Andrew Mclean, TVS.
Photograph by Brian Gassel, TVS

shared by both the convention center and the arena yet hidden from view to the adjacent Ocean Drive. The arena and convention center were both oriented toward Corpus Christi Bay, allowing pre-function spaces and much of the facility to enjoy great views. The arena was designed to be truly multipurpose and is used for a variety of functions, from ice hockey to hosting games for Texas A&M-Corpus Christi's men's and women's basketball teams. The renovated, expanded convention center includes 76,500 square feet of easily accessible exhibit space, 22 separate breakout rooms, a 25,000-square-foot banquet

hall and a 20,000-square-foot ballroom. The existing Selena Auditorium was a largely pre-cast structure, and the renovation opened the space up for natural light and views.

Aesthetically, the arena, convention center and existent auditorium were reskinned to employ the same materials so they appear as one continuous composition. A bold, landmark appearance was desired for the complex's front entry and took the form of an expansive façade of folded glass, making an

accentuated gesture toward the bay. The folded glass appears on the convention center and arena, furthering their seamless integration, and serves as a metaphor that the glass is battling the wind, which is abundant on the coast. Beyond the resplendent views, the profusion of glass makes the facilities radiate in the evening, informing those driving down Ocean Drive that activities are taking place within. The design also helped establish a welcoming, human scale with several large buildings, making access points more intimate in addition to making a grand expression toward accessibility off Shoreline Drive, which had previously been lacking.

The project has given Corpus Christi a dynamic complex that takes full advantage of the compelling setting and adds captivating and highly functional structures to the city's urban fabric. ■ ■ ■ ■ ■ ■ ■ ■ ■ ■ ■

ABOVE LEFT: Daylight fills the convention center entry lobby to create a warm interior ambience.
Photograph by Brian Gassel, TVS

ABOVE RIGHT: The convention center's glass entrance exhibits interior happenings at night to passersby.
Photograph by Brian Gassel, TVS

FACING PAGE LEFT: Metal and glass conspire to create a compelling front entry sequence.
Photograph by Brian Gassel, TVS

FACING PAGE RIGHT: The folded glass alludes to the typically windy conditions associated with such close proximity to the bay.
Photograph by Brian Gassel, TVS

Downtown Aquarium Restaurant & Entertainment Complex

Kirksey

■ ■ ■ ■ ■ ■ ■ ■ ■ ■ An eclectic destination offering something for everyone, Houston's Downtown Aquarium Restaurant & Entertainment Complex—a Landry's Restaurants venture—is a vibrant, must-visit component of the city's bustling downtown entertainment district. It was the skilled planning and design by Kirksey that transformed Fire Station No. 1 in the 400 block of Bagby Street and the nearby Central Waterworks plant into this one-of-a-kind amalgam of aquariums, entertainment, education, dining and enticing exhibits.

Using the shell of an abandoned downtown fire station, the design team took this 1960s-era building down to its concrete structural frame and readapted the building for a hospitality-themed entertainment complex. This included dealing with existing low ceilings, concrete beams and holes cut in the slab for fire poles, among other structural conditions. The nearby, historic Central Waterworks plant was reconfigured to host a 200,000-gallon aquarium filled with

FACING PAGE: Visitors enjoy a train ride that circles the Downtown Aquarium Restaurant & Entertainment Complex before taking them inside a shark tank exhibit located within a historic waterworks building.
Photograph by Aker/Zvonkovic Photography

exotic sharks. An additional consideration was the building's proximity to Buffalo Bayou, which required raising structural elements higher than normal to deal with flood plains and flood zones. From these rather disparate site elements an extraordinary hybrid entertainment complex was seamlessly fashioned.

The excitement builds for patrons to the Downtown Aquarium Restaurant & Entertainment Complex from the moment they approach the complex. An effervescent outdoor environment includes a 70-foot waterfall, fountains, plazas, a 90-foot Ferris wheel and a gas-powered train that takes visitors across the site and through the shark tank exhibition, all of which build a tone of exuberance prior to even entering the building. The ground floor is home to an exhibit of white Bengal tigers, an upscale bar and a 15,000-square-foot public aquarium. Collectively featuring more than 400 species of marine life and 500,000 gallons of aquariums, many of the exhibits are categorized into themed subdivisions such as the Louisiana swamplands, rain forest and Gulf of Mexico, which include regionally specific animals and information about their habitats. Throughout the complex biologists educate visitors about the animals, where they came from, conservation and other pertinent issues.

The second floor is home to the restaurant, which is set among a 150,000-gallon saltwater aquarium with reticulated rays, sawfish, sharks and other remarkable creatures. Within this space a 50-foot-tall cylindrical tank—the tallest fish tank in the world—is encircled by a grand staircase and is a focal point, climbing from the ground floor up through all entertainment levels. The third floor features a 6,000-square-foot ballroom that delicately blends a tone of sophisticated elegance with the prevailing aquatic theme. Outdoor terraces and wraparound balconies on the second and third levels afford extraordinary downtown vistas and are a popular setting for alfresco dining.

Impeccably designed by Kirksey from the shell of an abandoned fire station, the Downtown Aquarium Restaurant & Entertainment Complex has been a tremendous success, helping revitalize what is now a vivacious entertainment district in downtown Houston. ■ ■ ■ ■ ■ ■ ■ ■ ■ ■

TOP RIGHT: The second-floor restaurant, which can seat 400 guests, is a mélange of aquatic eye candy and savory cuisine.
Photograph by Aker/Zvonkovic Photography

BOTTOM RIGHT: The 50-foot-tall, cylindrical aquarium tank—the world's tallest fish tank—is encircled by a grand staircase and extends the full height of the entertainment areas to the third level.
Photograph by Aker/Zvonkovic Photography

FACING PAGE: The entry lobby to the restaurant acquaints patrons with the aquatic theme, which is reflected in the whimsical interior design.
Photograph by Aker/Zvonkovic Photography

Houston Baptist University Cultural Arts Center

Studio Red Architects

■ ■ ■ ■ ■ ■ ■ ■ ■ ■ ■ "Up to this point we have carried the chapel in our hearts; now, with the new building, our hearts are home." Donna Dee Floyd, co-chair of Houston Baptist University's chapel committee, expressed in her statement the excitement of the Belin Chapel and Recital Hall's addition to the Morris Cultural Arts Center on the university's campus. When HBU decided to add two premier performance spaces to its campus for the School of Music, it commissioned Studio Red Architects, a firm with distinction and experience in designing assembly and theater spaces, to create the momentous elements of the cultural center. Studio Red's project for the Morris Cultural Arts Center has generated a campus rooted in intellectual and spiritual faculties, as an interactive museum combines with a pair of acoustically refined theaters to frame the new and future student quadrangle, the university's first on-campus chapel.

FACING PAGE: The Cultural Arts Center creates a second student quadrangle and acts as a centerpiece to the Houston Baptist University campus.
Photograph by Jud Haggard

Adjacent to the landmark Hinton Center, a building patterned in traditional brick, the Cultural Arts Center utilizes the contextual material palette by complementing the existing campus' architecture with an aesthetically contemporary revision in brick and glass. Within the program of a 90,000-square-foot complex, a 1,200-seat theater integrates an orchestra, parterre, mezzanine boxes and balcony seating; a 365-seat chapel complements as a recital hall; a 14,000-square-foot museum displays important university collections; and a 7,300-square-foot grand hall and lobby connects all of these programmatic compositions. Experiencing the artifacts on exhibit in the museum was originally limited to Bibles from America's antiquity, yet these are now complemented with an addition of the history of America's South into the program, with relics of the Civil War including an interactive log cabin replica.

Engineering the acoustics of the theater and chapel to provide optimum listening experiences required design intentions concentrated on sound isolation, mechanical noise and vibration reduction, and sound system integration. Inside the chapel, an acoustical sound reflector suspended from the ceiling embraces a ring of discs and lights, projecting a metaphor of a halo above the crowd and serving as a centerpiece of the stage. This is surrounded by clerestory windows along the periphery of the building, which accentuate the lightness and grace of the campus architecture.

Studio Red Architects' design for the Morris Cultural Arts Center has provided Houston Baptist University with a long-awaited chapel and two technologically advanced performance venues. These additions have created an architectural program that emphasizes the unique quality of spiritual and intellectual endeavors encouraged by the university, completing a spiritually engaging academic campus. ■ ■ ■ ■ ■ ■ ■ ■ ■ ■

ABOVE LEFT: Expansive glass defines the entry, exhibiting interior activity to passersby.
Photograph by Jud Haggard

ABOVE RIGHT: The 7,300-square-foot grand hall links the center's various facilities and is capable of hosting a 400-person sit-down dinner.
Photograph by Jud Haggard

FACING PAGE TOP: The 365-seat Belin Chapel and Recital Hall provides professional-quality acoustics.
Photograph by Jud Haggard

FACING PAGE BOTTOM: Horizontal red striations stripe the 1,200-seat proscenium theater, which is an ideal space for hosting large-scale productions.
Photograph by Jud Haggard

Lady Bird Johnson Wildflower Center

Overland Partners

Lady Bird Johnson dedicated much of her life to promoting the conservation and use of native plants for their aesthetic, economic and environmental value. Simply put, this was, along with the University of Texas, her passion in life. Completed in 1995, the Lady Bird Johnson Wildflower Center has made an indelible impact, the effects of which transcend Austin, the Texas Hill Country and even the Lone Star State. In 2006, not long before her passing, Lady Bird witnessed the coalescence of her two loves, as her eponymous Wildflower Center became a part of the University of Texas at Austin, creating a synergistic union with incalculable long-term benefit.

Early in design stages, Lady Bird met with Overland Partners and was asked what her vision for the project was. Her response: "I'd like it to look like God put it there." No small task, the design team sought to decipher how the creator of the universe would honor the creation. A 40-acre tract of quintessential Hill

FACING PAGE: The Wildflower Center was designed as a response to nature and a model of conservation.
Project Design Team: Richard M. Archer, Robert L. Shemwell, Timothy B. Blonkvist, H. Hobson Crow and Jeffrey T. Russell.
Photograph by Timothy Hursley

Country terrain with gently rolling hills, cacti, oak trees and, of course, ubiquitous wildflowers provided an ideal canvas of ineffable grandeur. The design sought to model resource conservation, how to live on the land, how to respond to natural cycles of water, sun, wind, etc.—quite simply, how to respond to nature.

From the onset of construction, great effort was made to ensure minimal impact. A critical drainage way that ran through the site and contributed water directly to the Edwards Aquifer was not only protected but the water quality was enhanced. Hundreds of volunteers performed rescue plantings in the area, transplanting native plants to other locations on site. Trees were painstakingly protected, grasslands were valued as much as mature trees and all vegetation was protected literally to the build zone—the construction site was lined by a sea of vibrant wildflowers.

The structures reflect three regional vernaculars. Sandstone buildings recall the missions and structures built by Spanish Colonialists as they moved north; Germanic traditions redolent of Fredericksburg and surrounding areas are exhibited in simple limestone buildings with galvanized metal roofs; and a ranching vernacular is evident in buildings with corrugated, galvanized metal siding and galvanized metal roofs. The center was designed prior to the existence

LEFT: One of many environmentally friendly design components, this aqueduct carries rainwater to native plantings.
Photograph by Timothy Hursley

FACING PAGE LEFT: The sandstone lookout tower serves as a wayfinding device and is the center's largest rainwater cistern.
Photograph by Timothy Hursley

FACING PAGE RIGHT: Rainwater collected from the gallery roof is transferred via gutters to a cistern, where it will be used for irrigation.
Photograph by Timothy Hursley

of USGBC LEED and Austin Green Building programs, yet the architect comprised a thorough checklist of sustainable components and enacted them—the project is slated to receive LEED Gold certification via the LEED Existing Building program.

A large sandstone tower is a compelling focal point, affording an ideal viewing spot from above, and a valuable node. It also is the largest rainwater-collecting cistern on site, providing garden irrigation, and the core is filled with non-biodegradable construction materials. The checklist also incorporated

deep overhangs, the use of low-energy, recyclable and local materials, low water consumption and daylighting, among many elements.

An overwhelming success, the Lady Bird Johnson Wildflower Center has grown from 40 acres to encompass more than 300, with management oversight on more than 2,000 acres of additional land that would have otherwise been housing. And that is truly a legacy that would make Lady Bird smile. ■ ■ ■ ■ ■ ■ ■ ■ ■ ■

Moody Gardens

Morris Architects

■ ■ ■ ■ ■ ■ ■ ■ ■ ■ In the early 1980s the Moody Foundation sought to reclaim and transform a portion of Galveston Island that had long been used as a city dump—literally a landfill adjacent to the airport—into an attraction devoted to public outreach. An automobile accident to Russell Moody, son of foundation patriarch Robert L. Moody Sr., became the impetus for his involvement with hippotherapy, a treatment strategy that utilizes equine movement. This became the starting point to develop an arena and a place for horses, which started working with people who had head injuries as a community outreach. The original 120-acre parcel was leased and an animal contact facility was erected along with a white-sand beach for family interaction. It was the desire for something more of an attraction and the fact that the animals had outgrown the facilities that ultimately led away from hippotherapy to today's botanical and aquatic-themed complex.

ABOVE: The dramatic pyramids of Moody Gardens facing the Gulf of Mexico are unmistakable icons on Galveston Island.
Photograph by Morris Architects

FACING PAGE: Moody Gardens Convention Center's pedestrian plaza is heavily landscaped and intricately lit, allowing guests to socialize while providing protected passage to a new 1,000-car parking garage.
Project Design Team: Mike Riley, Douglas McLeod, John Zendt and Mark V. Martof.
Photograph by Mike McCormick

Upon entrance into Moody Gardens visitors are immediately surrounded by lush vegetation of myriad varieties. Three captivating pyramids are focal points of the complex and house distinctive areas dedicated to aquarium and penguin exhibits, a tropical rainforest and a discovery museum used for traveling exhibits. The tropical rainforest pyramid contains several varied environments found within the rainforest, which required a delicate balance of climatic issues related to the different ecosystems while maintaining a comfortable climate for guests. The visit begins with educational programs that teach about the rainforest and the need to preserve and protect fragile ecosystems, and any Moody Gardens visit is rooted in education. The aquarium pyramid brought the challenge of containing 2 million gallons of water in a defined shape, which also had to function as a refrigerated box for the penguin community—affording condensation and insulation complexities—while providing climates compatible with human presence. The third pyramid provides adaptable museum exhibit space for displays and other utilitarian needs.

Nestled among acres of tropical gardens and magnificent pyramids sits the four-diamond, full-service Moody Gardens Hotel, Spa and Convention Center. This architectural marvel features 428 beautifully decorated guest rooms, more than 22,000 square feet of flexible meeting space, dining, and a full-service salon and spa. Originally known as Hope Arena, the Moody Gardens Convention Center expanded from 35,000 to 100,000 square feet of combined meeting space to accommodate tradeshows, conventions and events. The center's exhibit hall is ballroom-quality with custom-made chandeliers and features state-

of-the-art sound and lighting equipment with soundproof walls and telescopic seating for 5,000, with total seating for 7,500 overall. The design features optimal versatility and the ability to convert from tradeshows to large ballroom galas, making it the ideal venue for all types of events. A 1,000-car parking garage with connected, covered walkways is another convenience added during the expansion.

From a landfill to a 242-acre educational and entertainment complex that is a requisite component of any trip to Galveston Island, the two-decade-long collaboration between the Moody Foundation and Morris Architects has given Galveston a multifarious attraction, the benefits of which are inestimable to the local and regional community. ■ ■ ■ ■ ■ ■ ■ ■ ■ ■

ABOVE: A project of immense scope planned over many years, the 242-acre Moody Gardens educational/ entertainment campus revitalized a significant portion of Galveston Island.
Photograph by Pro Aire

FACING PAGE LEFT: The aquarium's 10-story atrium entrance provides an aesthetic transfer to the marine world through the integration of materials, textures, color and lighting.
Photograph by Joe Aker

FACING PAGE RIGHT: The 2-million-gallon Caribbean exhibit features a 60-foot-long acrylic tunnel and viewing dome resting under 30 feet of water, which totally immerses the viewer for an incomparable experience.
Photograph by Joe Aker

Nancy Lee and Perry R. Bass Performance Hall

■■■■■■■■■■■■■■■■■■■■■■■■■■■■■■■■■■■■

David M. Schwarz Architects

■ ■ ■ ■ ■ ■ ■ ■ ■ ■ Arriving at two monolithic angels sounding golden trumpets that are reaching out over the streets, visitors might feel as if they have reached the pearly gates. Upon further review, however, it quickly becomes apparent that this divine iconography is actually ornamentation along the north façade of Nancy Lee and Perry R. Bass Performance Hall—a world-class performing arts venue worthy of such eminent grandeur. In a city that boasts the nation's third-largest cultural district, the David M. Schwarz Architects-designed Bass Hall has played the leading role in the revitalization of downtown Fort Worth and has given the Lone Star State an exquisite concert theater on par with centuries-old equivalents found in Europe.

Opened in 1998, Bass Hall represents the realization of a mission to create an illustrious, multiuse performance hall capable of serving the needs of Fort Worth's vibrant performing arts community, its educational goals and agendas, and its patrons. As the resident home to the Fort Worth Symphony,

FACING PAGE: The distinctive main entry façade at Commerce and West 4th streets sets the stage for the world-class performances that occur within.
Photograph by Steve Hall © Hedrich Blessing

Fort Worth Opera, Texas Ballet Theater, Casa Mañana Musical Theater and the quadrennial Van Cliburn International Piano Competition, in addition to serving as the premier local venue for incoming performances and traveling Broadway productions, Bass Hall is the focal point and centerpiece of Fort Worth's downtown.

Design architect David M. Schwarz Architects' initial foray into this illustrious endeavor was the result of undertaking a downtown Fort Worth master plan, which gave the firm great awareness of the site-planning parameters. The chosen site, within the Sundance Square neighborhood, comprised a single 200-by-200-foot city block, posing numerous design constraints. Creative planning and meticulous coordination were imperative to attaining the essential 2,000-seat auditorium size without compromising function or parking needs. The configuration placed the facility's rear up against an 11-story garage, while one corner of the front façade addresses Sundance Square's pedestrian activity and the other corner relates to two existing parking garages.

Aesthetically, the selected design pays reference to the Viennese Succession, a time period when many great classical pieces were composed, through limestone and stucco forms. While the overall massing is wholly compelling in its own right, two 48-foot-tall, sculpted limestone angels with gold leaf trumpets are unmistakable icons that define the exterior. Because the stringent site disallowed a large entry on axis with the auditorium, two corner entries were implemented, each of which is a multistory space connecting all different patron levels of the building.

The immaculate auditorium, the result of collaboration with world-class consultants, is acoustically superior; columns and wall panels were used to create dispersed acoustic reflections while also visually dividing the walls into smaller parts. Virtuoso Yo-Yo Ma described it as "one of those rare halls in which the music heard by the audience is the same as that heard by the performer. The clarity of sound heard throughout the entire range ... makes Bass Performance Hall one of the very best." The dome ceiling is painted majestically with sheltering angel wings and cloud imagery, furthering the celestial motif in what has quickly become the crown jewel of Fort Worth. ■ ■ ■ ■ ■ ■ ■ ■ ■ ■

RIGHT: Iconic marble angels adorn the exterior of the building.
Photograph by Steve Hall © Hedrich Blessing

FACING PAGE LEFT: The multistory entry lobby, ornamented with Texas flora murals, connects all patron levels of the facility.
Photograph by Steve Hall © Hedrich Blessing

FACING PAGE RIGHT: The majestic angel wing dome of the concert hall is truly captivating, and the wing motif is echoed in the end stanchions of the orchestra seats.
Photograph by Steve Hall © Hedrich Blessing

REEF

O4D Office for Design

■ ■ ■ ■ ■ ■ ■ ■ ■ ■ The realization of a hip new restaurant and bar offering inventive cuisine and absorbing ambience requires more than just a visionary chef or creative cocktails—it requires compelling spaces reflective of a strong concept. O4D Office For Design's transformation of an 8,000-square-foot Vietnamese grocery store and diner in Houston's voguish midtown district into REEF, a must-visit restaurant offering sumptuous, exotic cuisine, an urbane cocktail bar and a lively wraparound patio, all enjoying resplendent downtown views, captured the essence of chic in an exemplary urban design.

REEF chef Bryan Caswell, a protégé of the renowned Jean Georges Vongerichten, and general manager Bill Floyd opened this exciting new restaurant in June 2007 based upon an innovative seafood menu featuring seasonal offerings combining the freshest seafood with locally grown produce from

FACING PAGE: This former grocery store was renovated into a sophisticated restaurant and bar. The façade evokes waterfront buildings, highlighted by deep-sea colors and theatrical lighting.
Project Design Team: Lisa Pope Westerman, Brooks Howell, Caryn Mims, Le'Ann Whitley, Veronica Hernandez, Cedric Spears and Jasleen Sarai.
Photograph by Joe Aker

Houston's farmers' markets. Bryan's passion for fishing and love of seafood were the inspiration for this authentic market restaurant, and the design metamorphosis of an old building into architecture befitting of his uncustomary cuisine exudes a welcoming tone yet conveys this is anything but a typical seafood restaurant.

For patrons the intrigue immediately builds upon entry, as the foyer provides framed views into a market-style fish room, hinting at the delectable culinary creations being prepared in the kitchen. Eschewing cliché aquatic iconography such as ceiling-hung boats, nets and other hackneyed vestiges of maritime milieu, the interior color palette is inspired by the hues of the deep sea, invoking an array of varying tones of sea greens throughout. The grandeur of this room is enhanced via striking views to downtown expressed through voluminous windows. A wraparound patio further capitalizes on the serene vistas and enables alfresco dining when the weather warrants it.

From the entry vestibule the restaurant opens to an illustrious dining area with lofty ceilings and magnificent, pre-existing concrete beams. Sixteen shimmering capiz shell pendants hang from the ceiling above pearlescent tabletops, which gleam gently such as the inside of an oyster shell. Along the periphery a textured,

TOP LEFT: An encompassing view of the main dining room greets patrons upon their arrival. Shimmering lights and glistening finish selections soften the expansive concrete space.
Photograph by Joe Aker

BOTTOM LEFT: The custom steel wine wall provides a dramatic focal point against the background of a soft, textured plaster wall reminiscent of the sea floor.
Photograph by Joe Aker

FACING PAGE LEFT: The dim, murky feeling of the restroom corridor is achieved by lighting only the floor with blue LED fixtures, accented by a black-light coralarium.
Photograph by Joe Aker

FACING PAGE RIGHT: The "pearl within the oyster" concept repeats throughout, from pearlescent tabletops to the molded plaster "sea floor," lighted to cast wavy shadows above the banquettes.
Photograph by Joe Aker

undulating wall reminiscent of ocean waves illuminates and projects shadows above the banquettes. A suspended, 15-foot powder-coated steel wine wall flaunting more than 1,500 bottles is the focal point of this room and can be observed from any vantage, including an engagement room and private dining area. Contained within a glass-enclosed, temperature-controlled room, the wine wall is accented by theatrical lighting and an engaging foodie bar where chefs delight customers.

REEF is also home to the über-cosmopolitan 3RD Bar, which greets visitors with beams of light that suffuse the ceiling above, evoking the feeling of entering the space from below the ocean water's surface. An eclectic aura permeates the bar, emanating a vibrant, sexy mood that can afford the ideal backdrop for a business lunch as well as a trendy hangout for a stirring night on the town. Passage from the bar or dining area to restrooms is made through an unconventional, blue-lit corridor of cavernous proportions in which a black-lit coralarium lines the wall, exhibited like extraordinary gems in a museum.

An exciting young design firm that proved ideal to complete REEF's transformation into an unparalleled restaurant and bar, O4D Office For Design added a unique and bustling hot spot to midtown Houston. ■ ■ ■ ■ ■ ■ ■ ■ ■ ■ ■

Reliant Stadium

■ ■

HOK Sport

■ ■ ■ ■ ■ ■ ■ ■ ■ ■ Long heralded as a hub of technology, industry and space exploration, by the late 1990s Houston sorely needed a first-rate, multipurpose football venue befitting of such an eclectic, accomplished city. HOK Sport's design and implementation of Reliant Stadium, a high-tech, multifunctional facility embodying the spirit of Houston, played a pivotal role in the National Football League's return to Houston in 2002. Moreover, Reliant Stadium has given the city a premier venue that is home not only to the Houston Texans but draws a litany of top-tier conventions, entertainment acts and sporting events—such as the 2004 Super Bowl—all of which have been of enormous benefit to the local economy.

ABOVE: The multipurpose, state-of-the-art Reliant Stadium plays host to numerous events, including soccer matches.
Photograph by Mark Green

FACING PAGE: Reliant Stadium was the first National Football League venue with a retractable roof; this innovative element has been implemented at additional NFL stadiums since Reliant pioneered the feature.
Photograph by Patrick Bingham Hall

Fitting of Houston's progressive identity, Reliant Stadium employs a sense of the high-tech via abundant transparency, which is achieved through the use of a space-age roof fabric and widespread areas of glazing. The translucent roof skin and abundance of glass on the exterior exude a vibrant, alfresco aura to the facility's concourse areas and gathering spaces. This composition also ensures that Reliant Stadium radiates at night, and the circulation and energy of patrons inside become apparent outside the stadium.

Reliant Stadium's roof structure was literally on the forefront of stadium design, becoming the first stadium in the NFL to feature a retractable roof, which was essential to providing a pleasant patron experience

during much of the year. Built independently of the rest of the stadium to ensure timely project completion, the roof structure is comprised of a translucent, Teflon-coated fiberglass fabric that splits at the 50-yard line and docks over each end zone. The upper roof skin is comprised of BirdAir's Ultralux fabric, which allows 17 percent light transmission into the stadium. The roof fully opens in just about 10 minutes and creates an open area of 175,000 square feet.

The roof is supported by four massive concrete supercolumns at the corners, which support 1,000-foot-long supertrusses spanning the length of the field. The unique form of the steel trusses adds visual interest to the stadium's interior volume. Trusses also create rigidity for the system and support the massive scoreboard

and video board at each end of the stadium. The stadium's seating bowl is set remarkably close to the playing field, ensuring every spectator would be as close to the action as possible. In addition, a level of suites located below the club seats just off the main concourse provides the closest suites in the NFL.

Four club-level entertainment areas are themed and distinctive yet all reflect proud emblems of Texas to create an engaging experience. The football bar was designed in the shape of a football with an illuminated canopy over the bar creating the appearance of a football's laces, and custom barstools adorned in football leather reinforce the theme. A spur bar includes abundant maps and Western-themed upholsteries reflecting Texas heritage, and the star bar shimmers with brushed, stainless steel countertops

and translucent panels with stars representing famous Texans, including musicians, politicians, industrialists and frontiersmen. A horseshoe bar pays tribute to Texas ranches and famous cowboys, and as a whole, Reliant Stadium truly captures the essence of Houston. ■ ■ ■ ■ ■ ■ ■ ■ ■ ■ ■

ABOVE LEFT: Home to the National Football League's Houston Texans, Reliant Stadium is full of energy on fall Sundays when the team plays at home.
Photograph by Ed Massery

ABOVE RIGHT: The completion of Reliant Stadium was essential to the National Football League's return to Houston in 2002.
Photograph by Patrick Bingham Hall

FACING PAGE: Extensive glazing exhibits the vitality within Reliant Stadium to passersby from multiple vantages.
Photograph courtesy of HOK Sport

Shady Oaks Country Club

Gideon Toal

■ ■ ■ ■ ■ ■ ■ ■ ■ ■ Originally built in 1959 in the beautiful Westover Hills area seven miles west of downtown Fort Worth, the clubhouse at Shady Oaks Country Club was the hub of activity at an impeccable golf course. The club was also well known as the home course of golfing great Ben Hogan. When an electrical fire in 2003 resulted in extensive smoke and water damage that left portions of the building in disrepair, the decision was made to build a new structure on the existing historical foundation. Under the direction of Gideon Toal, the design for the resulting clubhouse afforded enhanced functionality and a superior configuration of spaces while bringing resplendent golf course views into the clubhouse for member enjoyment.

ABOVE: Abundant glass showcases the illuminated interior of Shady Oaks' clubhouse in the evening.
Photograph by Charles Davis Smith, AIA

FACING PAGE: Wood-decking overhangs and expansive golf course views frame the dining area.
Photograph by Charles Davis Smith, AIA

The catastrophic fire was followed by an earnest discussion about whether the structure could be cost-effectively restored or whether the club should build a new clubhouse reflective of high-end golf clubs of today. In the end, the decision was made to build a new building, but one that utilized the existing foundation and entry drive. Everything else, from the welcoming porte cochere to the terrace overlooking the golf course, was replaced. The new clubhouse design was one rooted in function and practicality. Originally, the clubhouse configuration contained all the member functions on the club's lower level while the banquet activities, which were largely used by non-members, were on the upper level with its captivating golf course and downtown skyline views.

In the design for the new clubhouse the dining facilities were moved to the upper level, joining more appropriately sized banqueting facilities. The club was also made more flexible in its new incarnation by allowing different spaces to be combined for larger events. Exquisite entry doors with inlaid turquoise handles as well as wood paneling from the original building were reused in the interior of the new building, reinforcing a connection between the club's beloved old structure and the new. The integration of old custom millwork into the new building creates a sense of the old in the new structure, and the wood adorning both sides of the building—on the porte cochere in front and on the large overhangs on the rear—ties the public and golf course sides of the building together. The clubhouse design is clean and elegant, outfitted with regionally inspired materials including Texas limestone and complementary brick, abundant glass with dark window frames and wood soffits with dark outrigger ridge beams for shading.

From the remnants of a classic clubhouse, Gideon Toal created a compelling new design that takes advantage of its extraordinary setting in a flexible and more functional arrangement that provides club members—and visitors—with an unforgettable experience. ■ ■ ■ ■ ■ ■ ■ ■ ■

RIGHT: Brick columns rhythmically support the wood deck porte cochere at the main entry.
Photograph by Charles Davis Smith, AIA

FACING PAGE: The entry celebrates the club's past by featuring striking wood and glass doors salvaged from the fire.
Photograph by Charles Davis Smith, AIA

Town Lake Park

■ ■

TBG Partners

■ ■ ■ ■ ■ ■ ■ ■ ■ ■ Austin has long been a favorite locale for outdoor enthusiasts, as the area's undulating terrain and abundant bodies of water afford many enticing outdoor destinations. Lady Bird Lake, formerly known as Town Lake, is a reservoir on the Colorado River in downtown Austin formed in 1960, largely to function as an urban park in the heart of the city. Establishing the area as a major recreational attraction, a system of hike and bike trails was built along the shoreline in the '70s, though the land surrounding the lake remained a largely passive recreational setting. More recently, the city of Austin commissioned TBG Partners to create a design that would revitalize the 54-acre park in an effort to offer more active recreational opportunities while maintaining and enhancing its natural beauty.

FACING PAGE: Surrounded by abundant open space, children play in Town Lake Park's interactive fountain, which features multicolored LED lighting and is comprised of locally quarried granite.
Photograph by John Gusky

A long-term project planned across several phases, the master plan incorporates pedestrian connectivity and vehicular circulation to integrate the park with downtown and nearby neighborhoods. Early project aspects were largely devoted to infrastructural components, which included the reorganization of on-site buildings, leading to the demolition of the City Coliseum, the conversion of the existent Palmer Events Center to a performing arts center and the construction of a new Palmer Events Center. The landscaping articulated transitions between the existing and new buildings and beautified the setting, while circulation patterns were enhanced for better safety and neighborhood connectivity. A fountain was placed at the front entrance, and a reflecting pond and terrace were employed to create a passive recreational area, in which the pond mirrors the stunning downtown skyline and the terrace provides space for art exhibits.

Steps were then taken toward further developing the park's green space. The design and implementation of a common lawn provided extensive open space for play and leisure. This oval-shaped lawn is bordered by a pedestrian promenade with different colors and patterns of pavers, organizing a number of park features while providing lucid circulation. A captivating fountain plaza with more than 100 choreographed

jets and LED lighting allows for active play during both day and night and is an exceptionally popular park feature. Accessed by a concrete spiral pathway leading to the summit, a 25-foot observation hill takes advantage of the location's resplendent vistas. Atop the hill a Texas map shows distances to other cities, but it is the panoramic views of the park and Austin skyline that are the allure. There is also a one-acre wet pond, which holds and treats stormwater runoff and includes terrace walls and three observation piers, while a children's sculpture garden is planned to give kids another vibrant play environment.

Future phases of the project will further beautify the area, better connect the park with the hike and bike trail system, renovate the Auditorium Shores performance terrace and add additional landscape elements. TBG Partners' planning and design for Town Lake Park has improved this natural setting and established active outdoor spaces in this one-of-a-kind urban park. ■ ■ ■ ■ ■ ■ ■ ■ ■ ■

ABOVE LEFT: Three observation piers reach out over the wet pond, offering views toward the walled terrace, the fountain plaza and Palmer Events Center beyond.
Photograph by Amanda Gillespie

ABOVE RIGHT: Backdropped by the Austin skyline, Town Lake Park fountain's 100 choreographed jets create a dynamic nighttime display vibrantly illuminated by colored lighting.
Photograph by TBG Partners

FACING PAGE: Native plants, trees and lighting line sidewalks to safely connect the park with surrounding neighborhoods, promoting both use and walkability.
Photograph by TBG Partners

Wyndham at La Cascada

Thorn+Graves, PLLC

■ ■ ■ ■ ■ ■ ■ ■ ■ ■ An ideal blend of resort-style luxury and upscale accommodations, San Antonio's Wyndham at La Cascada offers sophisticated resort residences in the heart of a vibrant city. Planned and designed by Thorn+Graves, the 100-plus-unit tower revitalized an important section of downtown along the Riverwalk and has encouraged the development of additional downtown residences in the nation's seventh-largest city.

Wyndham at La Cascada was designed largely to complement the adjacent, 46-unit La Cascada condominium complex, which was also designed by Thorn+Graves. The condominium complex represented the first residential high rises built in the Riverwalk area in decades and was successfully completed under the guidance of Lyndsay Thorn, Janet Howard and Mario Sanchez. The design sought to reflect the Alamo City's unique medley of cultures and resulted in clean lines evocative of the 1920s and '30s. The Wyndham tower sought to reflect the design of the first La Cascada tower, which had been built shortly before, but with the addition of subtle ornamentation. A stone base gives way to white stucco forms reminiscent of Spanish and Mediterranean

FACING PAGE: The La Cascada complex was carefully planned and sited to take advantage of its great setting along the San Antonio Riverwalk.
Photograph by Adrian Lipscombe

styles. Additional varying colors of stucco subtly emphasize shading on balconies, trim and other design details.

The two adjacent structures both sought to capitalize on their valuable location along the river. The towers were pushed out toward the perimeter of the property line, creating a wonderful courtyard between the towers and, essentially, an extension of the Riverwalk itself back up to Dwyer Street. The two L-shaped buildings were sited so that the taller portions are diagonal from each other; parking for both towers was placed on the first six floors of the larger tower to preserve desirable views to downtown, over the King William historic area and long vistas over southwest San Antonio. Beyond the resplendent views afforded in every unit of both towers, the side of the structure that is focused on the river incorporates a wall of glass, further integrating the context of the river with the property.

Just moments away from the Alamo and myriad downtown attractions, Wyndham at La Cascada activated an important area along the Riverwalk, creating a bustling pedestrian thoroughfare and an enchanting courtyard between the towers, and helped revitalize a portion of downtown San Antonio, spurring additional business and residential development in the area. ■ ■ ■ ■ ■ ■ ■ ■ ■ ■ ■

TOP RIGHT: Architecturally, Wyndham at La Cascada employs white stucco over a stone base along with Spanish and Mediterranean nuances.
Photograph by Adrian Lipscombe

BOTTOM RIGHT: Set in the heart of downtown San Antonio, the development features convenient pedestrian access to the Riverwalk and is in close proximity to an array of inviting destinations.
Photograph by Adrian Lipscombe

FACING PAGE LEFT: The courtyard between the towers overlooks the river and serves as an extension of the Riverwalk back up to Dwyer Street.
Photograph by Lance Dannhaus

FACING PAGE RIGHT: Transoms above the windows suffuse light into the interior of Wyndham at La Cascada's elegant lobby.
Photograph by Adrian Lipscombe

CHAPTER TWO
Urban Living

Urban living has been revitalized in many cities that had once lost much of their vitality to urban sprawl, resulting in a recharged ambience, buildings bustling about with activity and convenient access to downtown living and working. These pages represent the finest examples of how an architectural vision can transform and improve the landscape and quality of life for city dwellers.

The firms involved in these substantial projects—whether mixed-use buildings that combine residential units and retail space or multifamily residences cropping up in place of abandoned buildings or land—undertake not only the logistics of planning, creating and executing the design, they realize the impact their projects will have on the growth and success of their native cities. Residences like Architecture Demarest's Magnolia Hill, PageSoutherlandPage's Rice Lofts and The Hailey Group's Waterstreet Lofts are sure to impress.

The architects' diverse attitudes and thoughts behind their buildings may fascinate or even surprise. One aspect that weaves a common thread throughout these projects is the commitment to elevating the quality of life for many. Yet these projects also offer the opportunity to make their mark on their city's history. After all, the multifamily and mixed-use spaces will serve as homes and places of business for generations to follow.

Magnolia Hill, Architecture Demarest, page 90

The Conservatory at Alden Bridge, Meeks + Partners, page 86

Bienvivir Senior Health Services

■ ■

McCormick Architecture

■ ■ ■ ■ ■ ■ ■ ■ ■ ■ Deftly nestled into the eastern face of the Franklin Mountains, Bienvivir Senior Health Services is a reflection of the local culture, its setting, the mountain and the unique essence of El Paso. Eschewing the bland, institutional aura that characterizes so many healthcare facilities, McCormick Architecture designed this remarkable structure as a response to Rosemary Castillo's vision of the people and their lives on the west Texas border. Resembling a cliff dwelling of a bygone era, the structure seemingly protrudes out from the mountain, conveying the angularity of the mountain's rocks while reflecting its aesthetic grandeur in color, texture and form.

ABOVE: The architecture is reminiscent of an ancient cliff dwelling nestled atop the eastern face of the Franklin Mountains, as if hewn out of the stone of its environment.
Photograph by Fred Golden Photography

FACING PAGE: Peering down from the mountain toward the distant eastern view at early dusk, the 24/7 Alzheimer unit is a lantern to the city.
Project Design Team: Karl Krauss, Patrick Smith and Edward E. McCormick.
Photograph by Fred Golden Photography

Bienvivir's mountainous setting presented grand opportunities for the design, but also great challenges with the undulating terrain. Bearing scars from failed development efforts nearly 50 years ago, the mountain had a significant portion cut out before being abandoned during an economic downturn, leaving the site vulnerable to years of wind and rain erosion. A valuable infill endeavor, the three-level structure comprising nearly 100,000 square feet was set down into the cutout and then taken down another floor so that all three floors come out on grade; this was an important program element, as it enabled Bienvivir's elderly population to make their way outside at each level, which is invaluable in an emergency. Primarily composed of granite, along with other minerals, the mountain is a captivating assemblage of reddish, amber and orange rock, the colors of which are reflected in Bienvivir's abstract, exterior stucco walls of terracotta, ochre, papaya and other earthy tones.

As a facility providing comprehensive care to El Paso's frail elderly in accordance with the Program for All-Inclusive Care for the Elderly, Bienvivir enables senior citizens to remain independent and reside in their own homes and communities for as long as it is desired and medically possible. Rosemary Castillo, CEO of Bienvivir Senior Health Services, started the PACE program in El Paso, and by bringing this laudable effort to west Texas has made a significant impact locally, providing an invaluable community resource. Patient arrival is denoted by a cascade of tranquil water from the roof of the porte cochere that flows down into a serene reflection pond; the tilework throughout Bienvivir's corridors exudes the feel of a river. Both elements relate to water's vitality and, more aptly, the powerful Rio Grande River, which is an essential

RIGHT: The building's abstract massing reflects the rugged landscape in hues of deep ochre, mauve, burnt orange and dark coral similar to its canyon setting.
Photograph by Fred Golden Photography

FACING PAGE LEFT TOP AND BOTTOM: The building offers multiple outdoor living terraces and patios.
Photographs by Fred Golden Photography

FACING PAGE RIGHT: The sound of cascading water is integral to the arrival experience.
Photograph by Fred Golden Photography

component of El Pasoans' lives on the border. Three distinct daycare centers afford patrons a comprehensive array of services, all of which benefit from generous daylighting. Beneath the third-floor center for dementia and Alzheimer's, two daycare centers include welcoming activity rooms, one of which is known as primavera, Spanish for spring, and is complemented by a room named otoño, or autumn. Both rooms include a skylight array with 16 skylights painted individual colors; a variety of greens and yellows adorn the spring room while a spectrum of oranges to yellows dot otoño's luminous display.

An ideal response to the unique terrain and the lives and culture of a vibrant community, McCormick Architecture's design of Bienvivir Senior Health Services met community needs via locally influenced forms and aesthetics, receiving special national recognition from AIA and the American Association of Homes and Services for the Aging on this design for an aging El Paso community. ■ ■ ■ ■ ■ ■ ■ ■ ■ ■ ■

ABOVE LEFT: The otoño (autumn) activity space is bathed in natural light and color through a grid of deeply recessed skylights with graduations of color symbolizing its respective season.
Photograph by Fred Golden Photography

ABOVE RIGHT: The Rio Grande symbolizes the participants' heritage as it marks the path from the elevator to the daycare entrance.
Photograph by Fred Golden Photography

FACING PAGE: The provider's logo, a Mexican elder tree, symbolizes the center's goal to maintain the "evergreen" spirit of its participants.
Photograph by Fred Golden Photography

1305 Lofts

The Hailey Group

From the remains of an old warehouse used by a local grocer in east Austin came an eclectic collection of 14 highly flexible and spacious loft-style apartments, which represent the ideal balance of old and new. Designed by The Hailey Group, 1305 Lofts on East Sixth Street was the first adaptive reuse of a warehouse in the burgeoning Saltillo District of east downtown Austin. The units' anomalous composition creates a compelling dialog between the existent warehouse features and new residential components, making 1305 Lofts a truly unique multifamily residence in downtown Austin.

Originally a produce warehouse used by Guerrero's comprised of concrete masonry units and steel, the structure lacked any truly identifiable features save a prominent parapet at the front entry and fluted concrete blocks lining the building's perimeter. However, the structure was of generous proportions,

FACING PAGE: Converted from an old warehouse, these live-work industrial-style lofts are an integral part in the transformation of East Sixth Street into a transit-oriented development.
Project Design Team: Trey Hailey, Kit Johnson, Tracy Shriver and Steve Bellanger.
Photograph by Hailey Mar

which provided ideal dimensions—40 feet wide by 26 feet high—for two-story, walk-up townhomes, while the interior steel structure and raw, unfinished gray concrete masonry block captured the essence of truly industrial loft units.

After removing the rather bland parapet, the windowless box was perforated to provide requisite fenestration to introduce natural light inside and establish a harmonious rhythm along the street. Wonderful interior walls of concrete masonry were preserved, as well as open steel trusses and steel columns, all of which provided great architectural character. Because the steel columns were originally set during the building's former life as a warehouse, each column's placement was random with regard to the building's composition as lofts. Marrying the old warehouse components with the new residences was of the utmost importance and created an engaging contrast in the new townhomes. Since the structural columns were allowed to fall where they may, interior spaces are enriched by the incidental placement of columns—whether columns push out a stair from the wall, land in a bathroom or become a room partition, there are many ways that old and new mesh for an engaging, quirky composition.

An ideal residence for more artistically inclined individuals who prefer to work from home, such as artists, writers, designers, etc., the two-story units provide maximum flexibility and spaciousness—all residences include 10-foot ceilings on the first floor and 16-foot ceilings on the second. Moreover, residences average around 100 square feet of private patio space and none have neighbors above or below. Despite their industrial character, the units are warmed and refined by the presence of stainless steel appliances, Silestone countertops, a combination of antique wood and stained concrete floors, exposed trusses and ducts and many skylights.

Unlike any other multifamily residence in downtown Austin, 1305 Lofts reclaimed a brownfield site In a valuable adaptive reuse project, providing wholly unique loft-style townhomes in a growing district of Austin. ■ ■ ■ ■ ■ ■ ■ ■ ■ ■

ABOVE: Second-floor balconies characterize all of the front units and overlook East Sixth Street a few blocks from downtown.
Photograph by Hailey Mar

RIGHT: Exalted 16-foot ceilings on the top level and an open floorplan afford great spatial flexibility.
Photograph by Hailey Mar

FACING PAGE: The raw, unfinished steel planter surrounds the front façade and connects to a gated parking lot in back.
Photograph by Hailey Mar

The Conservatory at Alden Bridge

Meeks + Partners

■ ■ ■ ■ ■ ■ ■ ■ ■ ■ After passage through a grand boulevard-style entryway, brick paving stones lined by tall trees guide the way to a centrally positioned turnaround denoted by a large fountain evocative of Italian piazzas. Just beyond, a porte cochere signals arrival and precedes entrance into a majestic, three-story rotunda, from where attention is drawn out to the courtyard with its inviting pool, shade lounges, water fountain and putting green, and then farther still to an outlying forest preserve of pine trees. What looks and feels like an extraordinary five-star hotel is actually an exclusive independent living facility in The Woodlands known as The Conservatory at Alden Bridge, which is providing a superior retirement experience for seniors in an elegant and inviting setting.

FACING PAGE: The impressive entrance is designed to reflect the elegance of Mediterranean grand villas.
Project Design Team: Donald J. Meeks, Somkiat Petchsrisom, Marvin M. Myers and Norma Myers.
Photograph by Geoffrey Lyon

Set on 10 wooded acres, The Conservatory is comprised of refined one- and two-bedroom suites with luxury elements such as granite countertops, marble vanities, crown moulding, stainless steel appliances and high-end finishes. Reflective of Mediterranean villas, the Neoclassical architecture designed by Meeks + Partners combines rich materials like clay tile, brick and pre-cast stone in classic, enduring forms that exude a tone of affluence. The apartment buildings are set amid pedestrian-friendly streetscapes adorned with benches, ornamental lighting and lush courtyards, with forested preserve beyond completing the site's pleasing outdoor ambience.

The Conservatory boasts an assortment of compelling amenities that would be expected at an upscale resort or on a cruise ship. Within the 30,000-plus-square-foot community center residents can enjoy a multipurpose game room, business and brain fitness center, well-furnished library, 40-seat movie theater, a bistro and lounge area, barbershop and beauty salon, crafts center, fitness and therapy center and an opulent dining hall. On a daily basis residents partake in fine dining at tables set with white linens, enjoying gourmet cuisine and complementary wine presented on fine china.

As part of its mission to create a setting that encourages seniors to live an optimal retirement lifestyle, the community offers programs dedicated to improving residents' strength, flexibility, balance, mind and general health to sustain each senior's independent lifestyle. In addition to having dieticians and fitness experts on staff, The Conservatory offers an enrichment program for the mind, which uses Posit Science's Brain Gym program to stimulate brain-processing mechanisms to function quicker and more effectively, providing great benefit to participants' memory, cognitive function and quality of life.

Proof that independent living need not feel institutional or appear as stereotypical retirement housing, The Conservatory at Alden Bridge's blend of remarkable luxury, amenities and community makes it a truly one-of-a-kind retirement community. ■ ■ ■ ■ ■ ■ ■ ■ ■ ■

TOP RIGHT: Resort-style features include heated pool and spa, gazebos, gardens, sitting areas and a putting green. Centrally located amenities encourage residents to walk and interact with others, thus creating a social, active atmosphere where friendships are developed. This environment promotes a longer, healthier lifestyle.
Photograph by Geoffrey Lyon

BOTTOM LEFT AND RIGHT: Throughout the property, including hallways, decorative arts and painted reproductions of renowned works of art by 18th- and 19th-century artists grace the walls.
Photographs by Geoffrey Lyon

FACING PAGE TOP: With varied elevations, meandering pathways, lush landscaping mingled with water features, cultured stone, terracotta tile, roof tiles and classical detailing, the architectural inspiration comes from the unified uses of arches, balconies and timber beams to reflect the grace of the architectural style. Other design elements include rich brick, masonry, warm sienna color palettes, stones and arcades of slender columns carrying archers; rotundas, bay windows and cornices add to the visual impact.
Photograph by Geoffrey Lyon

FACING PAGE BOTTOM: Covered seating areas adorn the 26,014-square-foot community center's perimeter, offering direct views to the main courtyard.
Photograph by Geoffrey Lyon

Magnolia Hill

Architecture Demarest

David Demarest, AIA, has a flair for designing gracious multifamily residences, skills learned from experiences undertaking such projects throughout the country and as far away as the Lan Zhou, Gansu Province of China. Closer to home, the original plan for the Magnolia Hill townhomes in downtown Dallas, presciently devised by David's firm, Architecture Demarest, has been an overwhelming success. The simple yet unique loft-style housing, along with its integration into the context of the district's historically significant, pre-existing architectural vernacular, give this community a sense of place and belonging.

The area that is now home to Victory Park was quite different in 1995. It was home to the MKT railway lines, which later became the Katy Trail, a recycling center, a large, abandoned grain silo, a public housing project and the Magnolia Station apartments, which were converted from the Magnolia Petroleum

FACING PAGE: The Magnolia Hill townhomes deftly incorporate the various brick patterns and colors from the industrial palette of nearby Magnolia Station in an innovative form. Photograph by Steven Vaughan Photography

service center—hardly the most desirable location to build luxurious mid-rise town homes. David undertook the challenge of designing 20 industrial, loft-style townhome residences nestled in this gritty, industrial neighborhood. David, already familiar with the area from previous design work on the West End Marketplace, Market-Ross Place and the Brewery, spent two-and-a-half years developing what would become a model and catalyst for the future development of Dallas' growing downtown residential community.

David's passion for historic renovation and adaptive reuse came into play from the onset. Cues were taken from the historic neighbor, Magnolia Station, incorporating its industrial character into the new lofts. Architecture Demarest utilized a Victorian time frame and industrial-style thought process with the units, in addition to complementing various brick patterns and colors with the palette of Magnolia Station.

Inside, each three-story unit features steel frames, stained concrete floors and an infrastructure formed of heavy-tempered steel columns and beams protected by rust inhibitor, giving them a rich patina. Each unit's second-story, loft-living area features two stories of glass, providing stunning views of the downtown Dallas skyline. The open third floor overlooks the living area, enjoying spectacular downtown views, and incorporates industrial pine tongue-and-groove flooring. The units, all sold prior to the project's completion, have custom finishes and styling throughout; owners worked with David to personalize and individualize their respective loft homes.

From this innovative construction design, with clever use of materials and interior floorplans, Architecture Demarest designed townhomes that will endure, escaping association with any particular architectural

style or time period—he refers to them as "100-year buildings." To illustrate this point, most of the original residents still call Magnolia Hill home.

From a property that was so unappealing David joked he thought his father would disown him if he undertook the Magnolia Hill project, to the push for what is now a downtown residential community rife with growth, Demarest's masterpiece not only succeeded, but has flourished and will undoubtedly stand the test of time. ■ ■ ■ ■ ■ ■ ■ ■ ■ ■

ABOVE LEFT: Each unit has custom finishes and styling throughout as residents worked closely with David to personalize their interior settings. Interiors by David Sterns.
Photograph by Steven Vaughan Photography

ABOVE RIGHT: The open third floor of these loft-style units overlooks the living area below and features industrial pine tongue-and-groove flooring. Interiors by Alice Cottrell Interior Design.
Photograph by copyright Photography, Stephen Karlisch

FACING PAGE LEFT: The views of downtown Dallas from atop Magnolia Hill are simply sublime.
Photograph by Steven Vaughan Photography

FACING PAGE RIGHT: Each three-story unit is comprised of steel frames, stained concrete floors and an infrastructure formed of heavy-tempered steel columns and beams.
Photograph by Steven Vaughan Photography

Rice Lofts

PageSoutherlandPage

■ ■ ■ ■ ■ ■ ■ ■ ■ ■ Originally built in 1913, downtown Houston's Rice Hotel was an architectural gem, which unfortunately had been vacated in the late 1970s and fallen into disrepair. Exercising tremendous sensitivity to rehabilitate a local icon within its original, historical fabric, PageSoutherlandPage revitalized and transformed the hotel, which is listed on the National Register of Historic Places. The restoration of the Rice Hotel and its conversion into the Rice Lofts, a 312-unit apartment building, played a pertinent role in the revitalization of downtown Houston and brought a former jewel back to its full splendor.

The Rice Hotel was originally built in two phases, the first concluding in 1913 and the second in 1925, and also underwent a significant renovation in the late 1960s that left some indelible effects. During the early stages of the renovation project the design team uncovered many old drawings and plans, which were found both in the structure and in the Texas Room of the Houston Public Library. Because there were no current drawings of the structure, the design

FACING PAGE: The main lobby has been brought back to its original grandeur with refurbished walls and marble floors and the restoration of murals by local artists.
Project Design Team: John Cryer III, Arturo Chavez, Joan Albert and Randy Hurst.
Photograph by Joe Aker, Aker/Zvonkovic Photography

team worked from early 1900s ink-on-linen drawings. With ample knowledge of the building's original structural intent and architectural details, the designers strived to stop the deterioration process and restore the historic fabric while adapting the structure for contemporary usage.

The restorative process was integral and brought back many rich details from the original Rice Hotel. The marble floors and walls in the lobby were refurbished and custom elevators—which were adorned with mahogany finishes redolent of their original design—were installed to fit the smaller, existing elevator shafts. Other corrective measures included treatment of the exterior, patching of floors and the treatment, cleaning and repainting of all the windows. Lamentably, the late 1960s renovation introduced air conditioning for the first time, which produced deleterious effects on exquisite, decorative plaster coffers and crown mouldings that were punctured to hang ductwork. As much of this ornate plaster work as possible was repaired and the lobby ceiling was raised to its original two-story height.

A spectacular ballroom on the second floor was also greatly restored, providing an elegant venue for refined soirees. Beautiful arched doors on the second-floor terrace were brought back from opaque, limestone block panels; murals at either end of the 7,000-square-foot ballroom were repainted by a local artist; replicas of original seven-foot-high, wall-mounted plaster statues serve as column decoration; and 100-year-old birdseye maple was used for the ballroom dance floor and several apartment units.

The project team also uncovered and restored a basement-level swimming pool that had long been covered with a concrete slab, demolished an annex building to provide a 340-car garage with entry to basement-level parking, helped create a lively retail setting on the ground floor with 1920s-era storefronts and, of course, provided an array of sophisticated one- to three-story apartments. An architectural objet d'art rescued from longstanding decay, Rice Lofts helped revitalize downtown Houston and captured the essence of a historic property in an invaluable rehabilitation endeavor. ■ ■ ■ ■ ■ ■ ■ ■ ■ ■

ABOVE LEFT: Several living units were given high-level finishes, while others are more loft-like with exposed brick walls.
Photograph by David Lawrence

ABOVE RIGHT: The second-floor ballroom was restored to its 1920s-era design and has been a popular venue for downtown Houston events.
Photograph by Joe Aker, Aker/Zvonkovic Photography

FACING PAGE: The beautiful arched doors of the second-floor ballroom were completely recreated in accordance with the original Alfred C. Finn ink-on-linen drawings.
Photograph by Joe Aker, Aker/Zvonkovic Photography

TwentyOne24 Lofts

■ ■

The Hailey Group

■ ■ ■ ■ ■ ■ ■ ■ ■ ■ The design for the TwentyOne24 Lofts on East Sixth Street largely coincided with the unveiling of new commercial design standards from Austin city officials. Predicated on New Urbanist ideals, the ordinances sought to incorporate vertical mixed-use development and further densify existing transit corridors throughout the city to create veritable walls along such corridors. The Hailey Group's design for the TwentyOne24 Lofts was largely used as a model for these civic design guidelines, which were not yet finalized at the time, and the project essentially represents Austin's pilot for these wide-reaching urban guidelines.

Located adjacent to lumberyards in an industrial area with railroads, light metal sheds and various metal structures, the site had a strong industrial character, to which the building largely alludes. To break down the building mass into a more appealing scale, the design is broken into three components: a large,

FACING PAGE: The interplay between brick and stucco creates a compelling aesthetic.
Project Design Team: Trey Hailey, Kit Johnson, Tracy Shriver, Julie Wilson and Bob Shelton.
Photograph by Hailey Mar

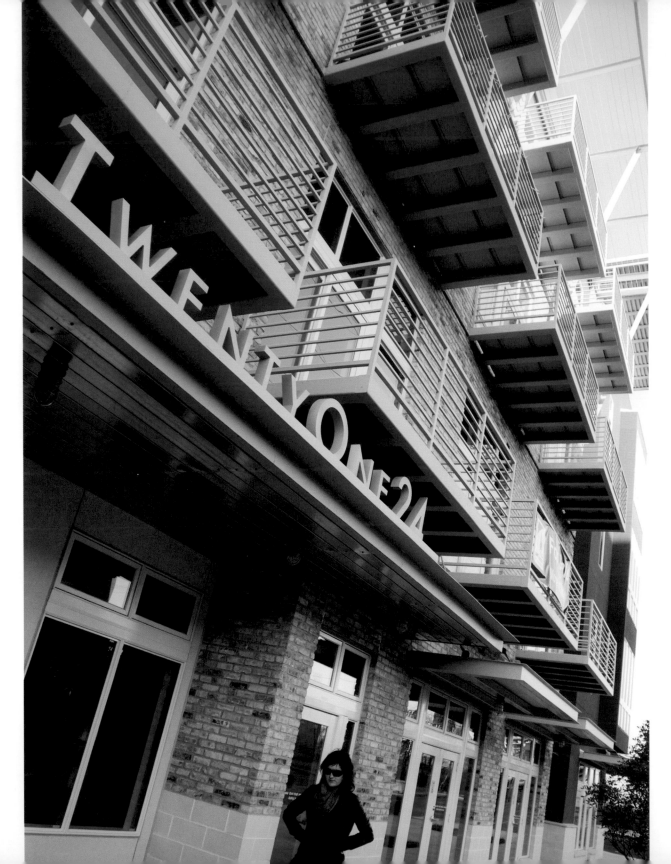

middle building sandwiched between more vertical bookend buildings. A steel-frame structure, the building has varied materials and dynamic architectural qualities yet steel expresses the structure via large balconies and overhangs, in addition to a thin, 12-foot cantilevered steel structure—a metal, hat-like brim—which juts out atop one of the bookends. Traditional and modern materials co-exist in the project, and collectively they represent the varied material elements of the urban neighborhood. One building resembles an old warehouse and is comprised of recycled brick, which adds character and a rich patina, while that form is contrasted by a stucco building with a modern aesthetic.

The design endeavored to maximize the allowable building height, 60 feet, as there were no proximate single-family residences. Throughout the development units feature approximately 11-foot-tall ceilings, as well as very deep dimensions with few walls and ample open spaces. The openness allows owners the flexibility to truly customize their interior space. Stained-concrete floors are low-maintenance yet elegant and further procure the desired loft ambience. Additional interior refinement is achieved through the use of marble, smooth sheetrock, concealed building systems, high-end bathroom fixtures and cabinets noteworthy for their clean, modern lines and barrel-grip hardware.

Creating innovative, loft-style residences from scratch in a newly built structure that exudes an old warehouse feel, the TwentyOne24 Lofts provide a brilliant model for the future designs of Austin's mixed-use urban neighborhoods. ■ ■ ■ ■ ■ ■ ■ ■ ■ ■ ■

LEFT: Large balconies and overhangs provide interest along the south façade.
Photograph by Hailey Mar

FACING PAGE LEFT: A 12-foot, cantilevered steel element, the metal hat-like brim juts out from atop the structure.
Photograph by Hailey Mar

FACING PAGE RIGHT: Ground-level retail beneath the residences animates the streetscape in an area with strong industrial character.
Photograph by Hailey Mar

The Villages at Samaritan House

■■■■■■■■■■■■■■■■■■■■■■■■■■■■■

CMA

■ ■ ■ ■ ■ ■ ■ ■ ■ ■ ■ For more than 15 years Samaritan House has focused its efforts on creating positive change for homeless and low-income individuals living with HIV and AIDS. It is one of a select few facilities in Texas providing a broad range of integrated services designed to enable residents to rebuild their lives and give back to their community. In late 2004 Samaritan House began planning for quality, affordable housing, located less than a half mile from Tarrant County's John Peter Smith Hospital, for low-income individuals and families affected by HIV/AIDS and other special needs. Designed by CMA, The Villages at Samaritan House opened its doors on World AIDS Day, December 1, 2006. This new facility tailored to a special needs community employed contemporary urban style to help spur redevelopment of an existing neighborhood within Fort Worth South's development district.

FACING PAGE: The mixed-use building includes a community room, offices and covered parking with residential units above.
Project Design Team: Bruce Carlson, Kris Calvert and Catherine Harvey.
Photograph by Charles Davis Smith, AIA

When the project began, Samaritan House was operating a facility consisting of 52 single-occupant rooms. The new design included renovation of the existing building and expansion to 60 units. In addition, plans for The Villages at Samaritan House called for adding 66 units, offering one-, two- and three-bedroom apartments in an urban village reflecting the unique character of the existing neighborhood. The urban village was developed by assembling adjacent lots within an older residential area. In the initial design studies CMA carefully considered the redevelopment goals for the area, researched the character of the existing neighborhood and selected materials to complement the existing urban fabric. The final design utilized durable materials and set the buildings close to the streets to improve accessibility and encourage interaction at a pedestrian scale.

The Villages at Samaritan House offers transitional housing designed to foster an independent, healthy lifestyle. The units provide large, open plans designed to comply with the Americans with Disabilities Act and to provide for the special needs of the residents. The exterior of the building conveys a contemporary urban image through the use of red brick, large-scale windows, a flat roof, metal awnings and projected balconies angled toward downtown. The service-enriched housing offers a variety of valuable programs created to promote personal development and well-being for the residents. One of the buildings includes a multipurpose community room located at street level, which is available for use by the neighborhood for a wide variety of activities. The facility also provides educational programs for residents, covering a variety of subjects including computer training, after-school tutoring, financial services and resume preparation. This building also houses the Samaritan House offices, leasing offices and residential units, set above the main parking plaza.

The completion of The Villages at Samaritan House created 100,000 square feet of new transitional living space, tripling Samaritan House's capacity and enabling housing and services for couples and families with children. For the first time in the agency's history, it was able to accommodate broader needs within the community. Completed on time and within the budget, the project has served as a catalyst for redevelopment of the surrounding neighborhood, and has helped Samaritan House expand its benevolent efforts to a vibrant local community. ■ ■ ■ ■ ■ ■ ■ ■ ■ ■

ABOVE: The urban design is expressed through red brick and metal on the façade, along with its close proximity to a main avenue leading toward downtown.
Photograph by Charles Davis Smith, AIA

FACING PAGE TOP: The development's 66 units come in one-, two- and three-bedroom varieties.
Photograph by Charles Davis Smith, AIA

FACING PAGE BOTTOM: Units feature large, open plans that were designed to meet residents' unique needs and comply with the Americans with Disabilities Act.
Photograph by Charles Davis Smith, AIA

Waterstreet Lofts

■ ■

The Hailey Group

■ ■ ■ ■ ■ ■ ■ ■ ■ ■ When designing a mixed-use development in a dense urban setting amid small-scale neighboring buildings, strong consideration must be given to how the scale and façades will affect the larger neighborhood. Add in stringent design guidelines from the city of Austin and well-defined programmatic requirements from the developer and the challenge becomes even more daunting. Adhering to complex—and at times, even contradictory—design guidelines, The Hailey Group's design for east Austin's Waterstreet Lofts reinforced the rich urban fabric of a redeveloping area with a large structure, prudently breaking down the massing to create a streetscape depicted as a collage of buildings.

FACING PAGE: Waterstreet Lofts features loft-style condos set above live-work commercial spaces on the ground floor of a flourishing development in east Austin.
Project Design Team: Trey Hailey, Kit Johnson and Richard Wilson.
Photograph by Hailey Mar

Working on a very small and dense site at the corner of Cesar Chavez and Comal streets in east Austin—a site that had long been a commercial corridor and home to historic structures—the first concept employed to maximize every square inch was to set parking underneath the building via one-story, tuck-under parking. An Austin zoning policy known as compatibility, which severely restricts height and clearly defines setback requirements in structures adjacent to single-family residential, also significantly affected the structural form. Comprised of a mix of commercial space, live-work units and for-sale residential units,

the development is defined by the three components with distinctive massings and material palettes, creating a veritable collage of buildings rather than one massive structure.

The structure is broken down into a contemporary, two-and-a-half-story component, a larger volume in the middle intended to resemble an old warehouse, and a building addressing the street corner, which is a shed form, redolent of the area's industrial character and seen in local railyards. The collective structure has a traditional composition with a pronounced base, middle and top, as well as shade structure similar to that of a cornice, yet its material palette varies with each component and is largely reflective of the area's existent character.

The middle, more-traditional volume is comprised of brick and concrete masonry, while the principal elevation along Comal Street is stucco and stone, accented by purple fireplace boxes protruding from the exterior with chimney flues rising up. Expansive glass presents a more modern aesthetic and takes advantage of the exceptional downtown vistas. At the nexus where the brick building and shed building meet there is a gasket at the entry, a joint between the two buildings, which articulates the pieces and expresses how they come together.

The unique building envelope and various zoning ordinances led to the serendipitous creation of eclectic and engaging residential units. Flats, lofts, open warehouse-style residences and live-work units vary but all have relatively open floorplans, affording flexibility in light, airy spaces. Successfully completed within challenging parameters, Waterstreet Lotts has strengthened this portion of east Austin's urban fabric with a historically relevant design depicted as a patchwork of robust forms. ■ ■ ■ ■ ■ ■ ■ ■ ■ ■

RIGHT: The open, steel-grate mezzanine and spiral staircase set the soft industrial theme of the loft interiors.
Photograph by Hailey Mar

FACING PAGE LEFT: The loft balconies facing the Austin skyline are framed by indigo-colored fireboxes.
Photograph by Hailey Mar

FACING PAGE RIGHT: The lobby entry is set within the architectural "gasket"—a node at which the brick structure meets the shed structure—which connects two of the building components.
Photograph by Hailey Mar

CHAPTER THREE
City Projects

Many city treasures are housed in public spaces, including libraries, churches, government buildings and educational facilities—or perhaps these buildings themselves are the treasures. The excitement of a weekly trip to the theater or the wonder a child feels stepping inside the cool interior of a museum surrounded by awe-inspiring works of art—these feelings are undeniably alive and guide the modern architects who commit their talents to these projects.

Whether the projects are entirely new, rehabilitative or for the purpose of historic preservation, there is a certain sense of grandeur and appropriateness that must be translated into the design plans—as is so eloquently exemplified in Casa Mañana Theatre by Gideon Toal, the Austin Convention Center, designed and engineered by PageSoutherlandPage over two phases, or the American Airlines Center, designed by David M. Schwarz Architects. Public spaces must reflect the city and the contemporary attitudes of its inhabitants while delicately integrating facilities and engaging aesthetics for all ages.

No city project is without its own set of challenges, yet those challenges offer the opportunity to create public buildings and spaces where knowledge, resources and enjoyment are readily available for everyone from the young to the elderly. Enjoy a look into what designers are developing for these city institutions and gain rare insight into their thoughts and inspirations for their cities through these projects.

Austin Convention Center, PageSoutherlandPage, page 126

Avondale House, Curry Boudreaux Architects, page 134

Julia Yates Semmes Branch Library, RVK Architects, page 154

A&M Church of Christ

Jennings*Hackler & Partners, Inc.

■ ■ ■ ■ ■ ■ ■ ■ ■ ■ Places of worship should remind congregants of their beliefs and elevate them to a higher level of reality, one in which the presence of God can be felt. Drawing on the beauty, thoughtfulness and symbolism of cathedrals throughout Europe, Bob Hackler, AIA, of Jennings Hackler & Partners coined "Texas Gothic" as the style of the 2004-erected A&M Church of Christ. A dramatically angled roofline directs attention heavenward, as does the grand glass tower with illuminated cross—a beacon in the College Station community, day and night.

Bob attended church at the A&M Church of Christ, while he was studying for his Master of Architecture, so he was aware of the needs particular to the denomination and the congregation. He and his team solicited the thoughts and desires of scores of people who would be interacting with the facility, from Sunday school teacher to minister. Dozens of questions such as "What image and values do you want to project to the community?" and "What

FACING PAGE: Striking rooflines and an exquisite glass tower define the church's exterior.
Project Design Team: Robert Hackler and Ken Jay.
Photograph by Michael Lyon

are the most important functional aspects?" returned a resounding consensus. In response to the desire for a friendly exterior that would invite visitors and welcome members, large areas of glass and many windows were incorporated into the architecture; respectful of the church's monetary restraints, the originally specified Jerusalem stone was replaced with brick, an appealing substitute.

With a large number of university students as members, functionally, the church needed to comfortably house 1,000 to 2,000 worshippers depending on the time of year, have a large central aisle for weddings and other ceremonies and boast phenomenal acoustics, conducive to congregational singing. In order to provide as large and open a worship space as possible, the architects decided to utilize a structural system akin to the flying buttress system found in ancient Gothic churches abroad to further enhance the majestic ambience. Once the architects had specified every last detail—from textile selection to pew placement—and the final result was unveiled on opening day, a woman approached Bob with tears of joy streaming down her face and uttered two simple, heartfelt words: thank you.

TOP LEFT: Clerestory windows bring in light from above the worshipper and also recall the high windows of the Gothic church.
Photograph by Michael Lyon

BOTTOM LEFT: The lid rolls back to reveal a floor-level baptistery, analogous to the traditions of New Testament immersions.
Photograph by Michael Lyon

FACING PAGE: Softened natural light is used to frame and highlight the worship activities and ceremonies conducted from the simply detailed pulpit area.
Photograph by Michael Lyon

This type of unsolicited response to a successful project is not at all uncommon for Jennings Hackler & Partners, which was founded in 1954 by Fellows of the American Institute of Architects and has experienced several iterations of principals of equal stature over the years. Almost unheard of in the industry, both Grady Jennings, AIA, and Bob began their careers with the firm; they so valued the opportunity to learn from people willing to share their expertise that they made the firm their own. Evident in their vision for the A&M Church of Christ, and the many other ecclesiastical and otherwise structures that bear their firm's name, the principals feel that the joy of religious architecture is "leaving behind something that inspires the worshipper and embodies the spirit of the congregation." ■ ■ ■ ■ ■ ■ ■ ■ ■ ■ ■ ■

ABOVE LEFT: The concourse was designed with extra width to allow the congregation to stop and talk to each other. The width will be essential as traffic increases with future additions, which are designed to plug into the concourse.
Photograph by Michael Lyon

ABOVE RIGHT: Designed to foster fellowship, all wing corridors lead to this large foyer.
Photograph by Michael Lyon

FACING PAGE: The large site was used to develop serene green spaces around the facility and separate acoustically from a busy freeway.
Photograph by Michael Lyon

American Airlines Center

David M. Schwarz Architects

The American Airlines Center is much more than an award-winning, multipurpose civic arena featuring first-rate technology and innovative sports design—it was the initial anchor of and catalyst for what would become Victory Park, the flourishing, 60-acre mixed-use development converted from an old railyard adjacent to downtown Dallas. As the design architect on this prodigious undertaking, David M. Schwarz Architects collaborated with an array of talented firms, team officials, civic representatives and others to procure the iconic design that now serves as the heart of the Victory development.

Stylistically, the structure was intended to represent a harmonious blend of traditional and modern elements; traditional to relate to the context of the immediate vicinity, particularly the brick-laden West End Historic District, modern to pay homage to elements of Dallas' more contemporary architecture.

FACING PAGE: The American Airlines Center's design established synergy with existent, adjacent neighborhoods and served as the initial anchor of the bustling, 60-acre Victory Park development.
Photograph by Steve Hall © Hedrich Blessing

The resulting design employs a palette of ironspot brick with limestone and granite detailing throughout while each of the four main façades features a large, arched masonry opening outfitted with expansive curtainwall. Each of these large openings relates to a barrel vault in the roof above, and these vaults form a groin to establish a distinctive roof structure with great character. The exterior is highly detailed throughout, which establishes a human scale that welcomes despite its massive size.

Designed to play host to the Dallas Stars and Dallas Mavericks, as well as large concerts and other local events, the structure has been an overwhelming success for all parties involved, and has added the Dallas Desperados football team to its list of tenants. The design team sought to establish a pioneering interior configuration that would be unlike most arenas, which typically have an oval or racetrack-shaped concourse that circumnavigates the outboard of the seating bowls with concessions and restrooms placed intermittently along the path. Four large lobbies were created, one facing each direction, that line up with the expansive curtainwall elements, so as patrons pass through the concourse they look out generous windows and have directional views to the city. These lobbies are linked to four rectangular spaces at the corners on 45-degree angles via flanking circular rotundas, each of which is open to above, creating five-story shafts through the building so patrons always know where they are in relation to other levels. Moreover, all concessions are located in the lobbies while the restrooms are designated to the four corner spaces. Treating the concourse as a true building rather than merely space between the seating bowl and façade ensured that guests are consistently aware of their location within the building and their relation to the city beyond.

As a result of the dedicated efforts to create a singular arena while paying homage to its contextual urban fabric, the American Airlines Center has been a remarkable success in all aspects. Designed and planned before the now-bustling Victory Park was established—and many of its elements had yet to even be masterplanned—this extraordinary public venue has truly shaped the city as it continues to grow up around it and has made an indelible impact on the Metroplex. ■ ■ ■ ■ ■ ■ ■ ■ ■ ■

ABOVE LEFT: Eight five-story-high rotundas located along the concourses inform patrons where they are within the building with relation to all other levels.
Photograph by Steve Hall © Hedrich Blessing

ABOVE RIGHT: A refined interior aura is established throughout, evidenced in the steel, terrazzo and aluminum lobby stairs.
Photograph by Steve Hall © Hedrich Blessing

FACING PAGE: One of four main lobbies, the south lobby features scale models of sponsor American Airlines' aircraft fleet throughout its history.
Photograph by Steve Hall © Hedrich Blessing

Andy Dekaney High School

■■■■■■■■■■■■■■■■■■■■■■■■■■■■■■■■

SHW Group - Houston

■ ■ ■ ■ ■ ■ ■ ■ ■ ■ Opened in 2007 to serve as Spring Independent School District's third comprehensive high school, Andy Dekaney High School is a grand structure with a capacity of 2,500 students in the ninth through 12th grades. In spite of the school's massive size, approximately 486,000 square feet under roof, the thoughtful planning and design by SHW Group, integrally coupled with the school's unconventional configuration into small learning communities, effectively breaks down the structure's scale, creating an engaging academic environment that students can call their own.

Dekaney High School is organized around four academic houses or learning communities, each consisting of students from all four grade levels. Upon enrollment to the school as freshmen, students are randomly assigned to one of the four houses and remain in that particular grouping through graduation. Likewise, each house has its own set of teachers well versed in the core disciplines and an administrative subset consisting of counselor, assistant principal

FACING PAGE: The site layout of Dekaney High School preserved the heavily wooded area; entrances and site signage were developed to create a natural park-like atmosphere.
Project Design Team: Mark Lam, William Wadley, Stuart Campbell, Jody Henry and Frank Kelly.
Photograph by Richard Payne, FAIA

and support staff. This organizational scheme enables students to develop long-term relationships with other students as well as faculty members via looping, as a freshman might have the same teacher for algebra one year, and in future grades levels for geometry, trigonometry, etc.

This configuration also allows teachers within the same house to collaborate and tailor lesson plans to overlap with instruction in the other disciplines. Within this smaller environment, students get to know their teachers and peers. The design provides a social gathering space within each house that serves as a student lounge as well as a flexible teaching space. The identities of these areas have their own unique and individual aesthetic, and can be easily viewed from the school's main corridor. This identity is created through the use of differing wainscot, trim work, doors, carpet and other finishes.

Beyond this unique organization, the design achieves an aura of welcome via an abundance of natural light and the prevalence of natural, low-maintenance interior materials. The main spine of the building consists of two-tier clerestory windows that suffuse the interior with light. Exposed systems and ductwork provide additional scale and interest. From the basic structure all the way down

TOP LEFT: Low-maintenance materials with clean and simple finishes, natural light, and exposed wood beams and ductwork achieve the comfortable aesthetic the school district envisioned.
Photograph by Richard Payne, FAIA

BOTTOM LEFT: Flexibility was also incorporated into the library—four small conference rooms are available for quiet study areas, district administration meetings or independent, small-group study.
Photograph by Richard Payne, FAIA

FACING PAGE TOP: The highly visible theater entrance includes a marquee to promote the events and celebrate the successes of the performing arts students.
Photograph by Richard Payne, FAIA

FACING PAGE BOTTOM: The theater can accommodate any high school or community production with a full fly loft, complete scene rigging, lighting catwalk and sound control booth.
Photograph by Richard Payne, FAIA

to the handrails, the level of finish is clean and simple; materials were selected so they will naturally patina with age. Galvanized steel handrails, steel stairs, concrete columns, wood-beamed ceilings, limestone walls, porcelain tile floors and other natural elements enhance the feeling of warmth and character.

The school's theater is centrally located, highly functional and of impeccable design. Wood panels and a limestone base around the periphery lend themselves to ideal acoustics. This 900-seat auditorium can be functionally divided into a smaller 600-seat performance theater with two 150-seat teaching theaters. These areas are separated with an operable acoustic partition, so that three separate activities can occur seamlessly at any given time.

Providing a comfortable and inviting environment for an exceptionally large student body, SHW Group's design of Andy Dekaney High School gave the district an enduring facility ideally suited for its academic approach based upon small learning communities. ■ ■ ■ ■ ■ ■ ■ ■ ■ ■

Austin Convention Center

PageSoutherlandPage

■ ■ ■ ■ ■ ■ ■ ■ ■ ■ Originally designed and built in the early 1990s, the Austin Convention Center was integrally woven into the urban fabric of the southeast quadrant of downtown, serving as a positive catalyst to a vital and previously derelict area. A decade later, lead architect and engineer PageSoutherlandPage revisited the project, expanding and updating the facility to meet a rapidly growing city's changing needs. The second phase further enhanced the center's street-friendly aura and responded to its urban context.

The initial design was set on a site encompassing four city blocks and sought to respond to its distinctive adjacencies and create an active street environment. Stringing all the public spaces along the periphery of the building helped create a village of elements, affording scale and activity on exteriors fronting the streets. Pre-function spaces, lobbies, reception areas and other functional elements were expressed on the outside via varying

FACING PAGE: The use of different materials on the exterior faces of the building helps to integrate a massive structure into the fabric of downtown Austin.
Photograph by Tim Griffith

volumes and fenestration. The façades took cues from adjacencies and altered the scale to respond to the urban context. However, throughout the convention center the architecture consistently invites people outside and takes advantage of dynamic downtown views.

While the first phase occupied four city blocks, the expansion sought to double the size yet only had an additional two blocks available. Moreover, convention center needs had grown with Austin's growth, as the high-tech industry in particular had arrived and required increased functionality. By that time South by Southwest had grown into a major annual event, which called for ample performance space. The project team also foresaw the potential use as a sports venue, and added pull-out bleachers to accommodate such activities, and sure enough the Austin Toros basketball team now uses the facility for its home games. The integration of art added many layers of richness to the facility, including a collaboration with New York artist Jamie Carpenter on a captivating blue glass screen facing Trinity Street where the wall becomes part photovoltaics, part art, solar shading for the room inside and is a striking composition.

Laudable sustainable design concepts were employed from the outset, many of which were well ahead of their time—years before the existence of the LEED or Austin Green Building programs. The first phase incorporated active solar collectors, which were upgraded with new photovoltaic technologies during the second phase. Both phases took advantage of off-cycle electricity—which is otherwise largely wasted—to make ice at night, which was then used to air condition the building during the day. Since convention centers experience rapidly changing user groups—a handful of people set up exhibits prior to

conventions—ventilation was carefully designed so that the building could be kept a comfortable level for smaller populations without using the entire heavy-duty air conditioning system.

PageSoutherlandPage's efforts on the Austin Convention Center have made a tremendous impact on an important sector of downtown and the later expansion refined the technology and functionality of an integral part of Austin. ■ ■ ■ ■ ■ ■ ■ ■ ■ ■

ABOVE LEFT: A curtainwall of glass is literally hung from the roof structure; the frame and skin of the building weave together in a complex, interdependent and efficient manner.
Photograph by Marko Garafulic

ABOVE RIGHT: Vertical piers along the outside edges of the pavilion are comprised of a concrete base, a braced steel column and a branching tree of struts at the top.
Photograph by Marko Garafulic

FACING PAGE: The tour de force of the building is a large glass screen wall, which provides sun shading and solar energy collection in an artistic way.
Photograph by Greg Hursley

Austin Police Substation and Forensics Science Center

TAG International

■ ■ ■ ■ ■ ■ ■ ■ ■ ■ When a bond election passed approving the construction of a new substation and forensics science center for the Austin Police Department, TAG International was selected to design an appealing yet highly secure facility that combines disparate functions in a pleasant, cohesive working environment. The new substation and forensics center has given the APD an enhanced public identity, invaluable scientific resources and a state-of-the-art facility that meets its varied administrative needs—all while being completed on time and under budget.

Replacing an old ironworks building that had long been a neighborhood blemish, the 78,000-square-foot facility was designed to convey a welcoming, professional image to the surrounding community. The forensics center commands 50,000 square feet of the project, while the police substation and public areas comprise the remainder of the center. The desire for an exterior aesthetic that would reflect Austin's natural setting resulted in three distinct

FACING PAGE: Reflective of Austin's natural setting, three distinct material palettes define the forensics building on the left, public space in the middle and police station to the right.
Project Design Team: Ron Pope and David Carson.
Photograph by Greg Hursley

material palettes to define the three disparate program elements. The forensics portion of the center features a combination of smooth, burnished block with stucco and cast-stone accents arranged in an orderly pattern. The substation is characterized by a split-face block with a galvanized metal roof, while the shared public areas are marked by a galvanized steel canopy entrance, sandstone walls and curtainwall glazing. An inviting public lobby reflects a warm environment with a combination of cherry wood paneling, terrazzo floors, daylighting and decorative ceiling elements. A large community meeting room accessible from the lobby is used for public outreach functions and neighborhood events, as well as police briefings. This room can also double as a secondary emergency operations center when needed.

An extraordinary forensics scientific center provides APD with innovative technologies and cutting-edge equipment including a DNA lab, blood spatter room—a completely washable room used for crime scene reconstruction—photo studio, fingerprint analysis center, and a second-floor firing range with a 70-foot-long fire lane encased in a concrete structure. Housing the firing range, which emits significant vibration, and the DNA labs, which use highly sensitive equipment, in the same facility presented unique challenges; however, TAG's design approach successfully integrated these varied functions. Natural daylight is brought into almost every occupied space throughout the facility. Gallery

TOP LEFT: The public lobby features terrazzo flooring, cherry wood wall paneling and a public information kiosk with integral seating.
Photograph by Greg Hursley

BOTTOM LEFT: The forensics laboratories were designed to meet highly technical requirements while providing abundant natural light and views to the outside for a comfortable working enviornment.
Photograph by Greg Hursley

FACING PAGE: The galvanized canopy has become a neighborhood landmark that reflects the friendly, welcoming presence of the APD in the neighborhood.
Photograph by Greg Hursley

corridors allow escorted visitors to tour the facility and view the labs and firing range without compromising safety or security.

Security was a major design priority, with the goal of achieving a high level of threat resistance without projecting an unwelcoming image. Many passive security strategies were utilized to deliver heightened security without diminishing the center's friendly presence in the neighborhood. All exterior walls were made bullet-resistant by filling the concrete block with solid concrete grout and placing steel plates behind stone walls. The building was sited to eliminate runways and prevent vehicles from accelerating and striking the facility. Air intakes throughout were carefully protected behind secure areas to eliminate opportunities for airborne attacks through the building's mechanical systems. Landscape features were also designed to protect the facility through the utilization of berms as further vehicle impediments.

Austin was the first city in Texas to mandate works of art to accompany city construction projects. As a part of Austin's "Art in Public Places" program, a unique work of art adorns the front of the facility: a collection of native plants arranged in the shape of a fingerprint. A team of artists crafted this labyrinth of spiraling metal-clad planters that change with the season. TAG's design team worked closely with the artists in a collaborative effort to integrate the art with the landscape and building design.

With a design that exceeded the department's programmatic needs through seamless implementation, TAG International delivered an invaluable, recognizable facility that is functional, secure and community-friendly. ■ ■ ■ ■ ■ ■ ■ ■ ■ ■

Avondale House

■ ■

Curry Boudreaux Architects

■ ■ ■ ■ ■ ■ ■ ■ ■ At a school where the students major in miracles, the facility not only responds to the student body's unique needs but celebrates them—and the patterning and exterior character, which were derived from the children's art, create an aesthetic evocative of their remarkable perspective.

Autism is a complex and challenging neurological disorder that uniquely affects afflicted individuals. Avondale House is a nonprofit agency founded in 1976 by parents of children with autism to provide better educational opportunities for their kids beyond regular school districts. Growing from a small operation in a house on Houston's Avondale Street to a much larger entity serving several area school districts, the organization had a substantial need for a new facility to call its own. Designed by Curry Boudreaux Architects, the 35,000-square-foot Avondale House has given the foundation a much-needed facility that responds to the distinct needs of a special community.

FACING PAGE: The 35,000-square-foot Avondale House affords enhanced educational opportunities for children with autism in a structure responsive to a special community's unique needs.
Photograph by Geoffrey Lyon

The site, bounded by a residential street in southwest Houston, dictated a long, linear organization, which allowed for an excellent layout of the classroom space, accommodated an efficient drive area for buses and established a strong front-entry presence for public access to the building. Working on a tight budget, the structure called for fairly standard materials, but incorporating them in an atypical manner helped achieve the goal of a statement building that eschews bland, undifferentiated architecture. The rear, rigid-frame portion of the building is placed along the back property due to site characteristics, while the front piece is comprised of tilt-wall concrete panels.

Rather than simply painting the concrete panels, the architect stained the natural concrete, creating colorful, rectilinear patterns in an ad hoc grid inspired by artwork from the kids. The art affected how and where color was applied, as well as the fenestration, and ultimately symbolizes the different shapes, colors and spatial relationships contained within the mind of an autistic child. Asymmetrical patterns of glass produce a variety of visual effects, and represent the notion that these children see different images in almost a fractured, rectilinear kaleidoscope.

The design endeavored to create a healthy environment responsive to autism's particular needs, which included the use of low-contrast interior colors, private restrooms, durable materials and other considerations. Daylighting was an important component of the design, and while natural light is energy efficient and a vital resource, light quality was emphasized, as overabundant or misplaced light sources could be distracting to these light-sensitive individuals. A muted interior color palette was applied to aid students' ability to concentrate. Linoleum floors and natural materials reduce off-gassing and create a healthier environment.

As part of the redevelopment of this part of southwest Houston, Avondale House is a vibrant destination for a long-neglected area. It has also provided this laudable foundation with long-needed academic facilities that students can truly call their own. ■ ■ ■ ■ ■ ■ ■ ■

ABOVE LEFT: Natural concrete panels were stained to create vibrant, rectilinear patterns in an asymmetrical grid that was inspired by artwork from Avondale House students.
Photograph by Geoffrey Lyon

ABOVE RIGHT: The structure's color and fenestration symbolize the various shapes, colors and spatial relationships perceived within the mind of an autistic child.
Photograph by Geoffrey Lyon

FACING PAGE: Set on a site with broad street frontage, the building was designed to allow for safe and efficient drop-offs and pick-ups by school buses and vans.
Photograph by Geoffrey Lyon

Carl Wunsche Sr. High School

■ ■

SHW Group - Houston

■ ■ ■ ■ ■ ■ ■ ■ ■ ■ Carl Wunsche Sr. High School is an innovative career academy in which students are selected through an application process to receive opportunities for enhanced academic and career success via integrated studies, workplace learning activities, internships and cooperative learning programs. While the original structure was the oldest high school in the Spring ISD and had undergone numerous ad hoc transformations over the years, SHW Group's renovation and addition to the campus enabled the school to achieve its academic goals in a flexible, first-rate, technologically advanced environment that engages students and deftly integrates core academic and career programs.

ABOVE: The vision of Wunsche was to make instruction more meaningful, relevant and engaging by integrating core academics with the career and technology interests of the students.
Photograph by Richard Payne, FAIA

FACING PAGE: The architectural features of the facility respect the character of the adjacent Old Town Spring area, while at the same time project a professional, business-oriented image.
Project Design Team: Mark Lam, William Wadley, Stuart Campbell, Matthew Gvist and Frank Kelly.
Photograph by Richard Payne, FAIA

The existing school was surrounded by mature oak trees on the 22-acre site. As requested by the community, careful consideration was taken to preserve the existent trees and vegetation, which procured the unique layout of the floorplan. This layout, further reinforced by the placement of the entrance, led to the school's most captivating architectural feature, a two-story curved wall of glass that attains the desired high-tech, business-like ambience for the school. This glass wall is interrupted by towers clad in limestone, which is evocative of Old Town Spring's pastoral character.

The school is designed around three academic towers that focus on specialized areas of study that encompass professional, technological and medical programs. Two of the three academies are centrally located with ultra-flexible, two-story open volumes surrounded by core program areas; because the needs of the programs could change significantly, the spaces had to remain modifiable. Raised computer floors, adjustable data and electrical devices, wireless technology, and landscape office furniture were utilized for maximum adaptability. An elevated corridor separated by glass walls abuts this space to further promote interest between the available programs. Unlike most schools where classrooms are largely opaque, every room in the building features expansive glass, to reinforce the integration of core and career studies—creating an interactive environment in which student activities are proudly exhibited.

TOP LEFT: The highly flexible, two-story open spaces have extensive areas of glass so that everyone in the school may see the interesting work underway.
Photograph by Richard Payne, FAIA

BOTTOM LEFT: The majority of student traffic and social life takes place on "Learning Street," which links all major activity areas in the school.
Photograph by Richard Payne, FAIA

FACING PAGE: High-performance insulated glazing is used on the exterior, resulting in considerable energy savings and generous natural light in learning spaces.
Photograph by Richard Payne, FAIA

Providing invaluable career training that is limited or unavailable at most high schools, Wunsche includes professional-level facilities for its student body. Unique features include: a commercial kitchen for culinary arts; a court room for pre-law and legal studies; a licensed daycare center; a media technology/television studio; a functioning branch of a local credit union run by the finance students; a veterinary clinic; a medical clinic; a dental lab complete with dental chairs and equipment; an auto-technologies garage converted from the existing gymnasium; a small museum featuring relics from the original school; a coffee shop run by the students; and a first-rate fitness center that rivals a standalone health club. Providing this mélange of necessary functions all in one progressive learning environment, the ambience at Wunsche is truly one of a small city and its requisite service offerings.

SHW Group's planning and design for Carl Wunsche Sr. High School gave the district a dynamic learning environment that feels more like a business than a traditional school and has fostered an invaluable relationship between the school, local businesses and the community to the benefit of the students and the community alike. ■ ■ ■ ■ ■ ■ ■ ■ ■ ■

Casa Mañana Theatre

Gideon Toal

■ ■ ■ ■ ■ ■ ■ ■ ■ ■ Originally constructed in 1958 from an Alcoa kit of parts in 114 days, Casa Mañana Theatre has long been a distinctive component of Fort Worth's vibrant cultural district. The theatre was well known for its remarkable theatre-in-the-round contained within a stunning aluminum geodesic dome. While still a performance venue that hosts theatrical productions, Casa Mañana has increasingly shifted its emphasis to education and children's productions over the years, and its configuration as an arena theatre did not afford ideal opportunities for teaching the craft. After a decade of careful planning and fundraising, Casa Mañana received long-needed enhancements under the direction of Gideon Toal in 2003 that, most notably, converted the theatre-in-the-round to a more functional proscenium-style configuration, revitalizing the facility while maintaining its rich character.

Housed in one of the few remaining aluminum geodesic domes in the United States, Casa Mañana's theatre-in-the-round enabled great intimacy between performers and audience, but with no backstage area, actors and stagehands had to use the surrounding concourse and aisles to move set

FACING PAGE: Casa Mañana's new addition frames and connects seamlessly to the original structure.
Photograph by Charles Davis Smith, AIA

pieces, props and other items to and from the stage. Although the reconfiguration removed approximately 800 often-unused seats, it helped aid and enhance performers' efforts and provided additional space for Casa Mañana's nationally recognized educational programs as well as space for meetings and other events by the community. Concrete slab was utilized over the steel framing, creating the proper house rake, while a truss system above the flytower-less stage supports lighting, sound and rigging. The project also greatly increased the size of the lobby and added many adequate, accessible restrooms that had been sorely lacking.

Set at the prominent intersection of Lancaster Avenue and University Drive, a rather bland façade fronted this junction, giving Casa Mañana little presence and representing a lost opportunity. During the course of the project, design guidelines were identified and implemented to create better circulation and accessibility and to give the facility more visibility. The reorientation presented a large, transparent volume to the intersection, exhibiting activities within to passersby. An existent entrance off University was also closed, mitigating routine traffic congestion and making all vehicles arrive from Lancaster. This enabled passengers to be dropped off curbside rather than have to cross in front of vehicles, and permitted school buses to drop children off curbside as well. Circulation patterns from the parking area were rerouted to the front of the building rather than the back, which had long been the case.

Gideon Toal's renovation greatly enhanced the functionality and presence of a historic gem in Fort Worth, providing Casa Mañana with a flexible and enhanced performance space with greater accessibility and amenities without harming its structural integrity. ■ ■ ■ ■ ■ ■ ■ ■ ■ ■

ABOVE LEFT: The lobby reflects the circular plan of the original theatre and its generous size allows for increased pre-function and concessions.
Photograph by Charles Davis Smith, AIA

ABOVE RIGHT: The theatre interior now features a proscenium stage while still being sensitive to the much-beloved original ceiling structure.
Photograph by Charles Davis Smith, AIA

FACING PAGE TOP: Glass walls of the lobby provide views of the surrounding cultural district while sun shades protect the space from the bright Texas sun.
Photograph by Charles Davis Smith, AIA

FACING PAGE BOTTOM: Rhythmic supports and the sweeping, covered entry welcome patrons to the theatre's ticketing windows and main entry.
Photograph by Charles Davis Smith, AIA

Fellowship of The Woodlands

Studio Red Architects

In late 2005 Fellowship of The Woodlands commissioned Studio Red Architects to help master plan a significantly expanded and compelling campus that would display a tone of warmth and welcome. The resultant design, which was completed ahead of schedule and within budget, gave the congregation a complex of highly functional and engaging structures tied together with a palette of natural materials. It also included vibrant outdoor spaces for recreation or tranquil leisure and an immaculate chapel in the woods against which storybook weddings regularly unfold. The project included a 120,000-square-foot structure for children's education and worship; administrative offices; multiple auditoriums; a 15,000-square-foot, state-of-the-art bookstore; and a café with indoor and outdoor seating that is tied to an engaging outdoor fellowship plaza highlighted by a prayer fountain with a 30-foot-tall cross in a pool of water, used for baptism. But the jewel piece of the entire campus is undoubtedly the majestic chapel in the woods.

FACING PAGE: Expansive transparency brings the heavily wooded setting inside the graceful chapel in the woods.
Photograph by Richard Payne, FAIA

Secluded from the rest of the campus, the 450-person chapel is stunning and affords an ethereal setting for weekend services, weddings, funerals and other gatherings. During the conceptual design stage, it was Pastor Kerry Shook's wife, Chris, who noted that while Gothic-style cathedrals from centuries past are always grandiose, captivating structures, they are currently often austere and lifeless within. So the desire was to take that beauty, grandness and the welcoming quality of those structures and at the same time create a life and a light inside the structure that would be very bright and welcoming—a place for all sorts of different spiritual milestones.

Inspired by Faye Jones' masterpiece Thorncrown Chapel in Eureka Springs, Arkansas, the chapel blends graciously into its heavily wooded setting. The exterior is comprised of cedar siding and expansive glass, as both the front and back walls are wholly transparent. These façades were oriented away from the sunlight and a unique 40-foot-tall by 30-foot-wide MechoShade device ensures ideal lighting for filming even on cloudless days. The facility includes first-rate technology such as plasma screens, which are concealed from view when not in use, accommodating the needs of modern-day weddings while maintaining the chapel's aesthetic purity. Interior spaces are airy and free-flowing, further warmed by abundant wood

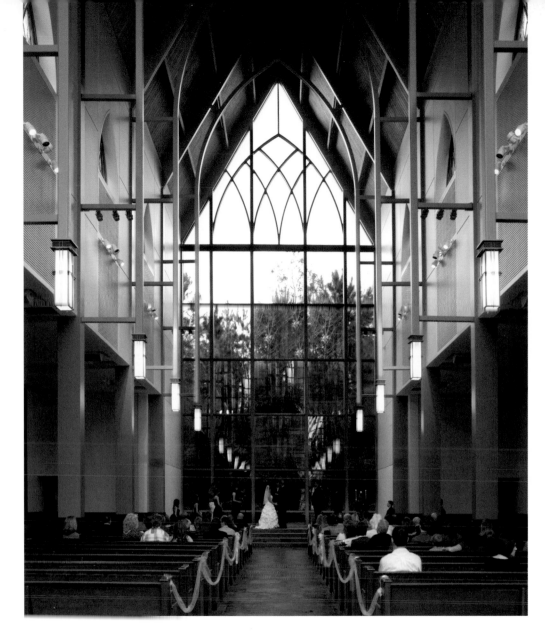

veneers, natural cherry wood pews, slate flooring and abstract stained glass. A 70-foot-tall structure, the

two side components of the massing step down to make the chapel appear even taller, lifting eyes to

the heavens. This simple, elegant design takes advantage of the site, adding to the serene and reflective

atmosphere, and the chapel was booked solid every weekend the first year it opened.

Exceeding the congregation's needs, Studio Red's planning and design yielded a majestic chapel and

compelling campus for a dynamic church. ■ ■ ■ ■ ■ ■ ■ ■ ■ ■

ABOVE LEFT: Slate floors and cherry wood pews enhance the chapel's rich, natural aesthetic.
Photograph by Richard Payne, FAIA

ABOVE RIGHT: Soft lighting fills the chapel at dusk, exhibiting the structure's grand symmetrical forms.
Photograph by Richard Payne, FAIA

FACING PAGE: The abstract stained glass and wood ceiling add richness to the space.
Photograph by Richard Payne, FAIA

Ismaili Jamatkhana

Hidell & Associates Architects, Inc.

■ ■ ■ ■ ■ ■ ■ ■ ■ ■ "The Center will be a place of peace, humility, reflection and prayer... It will be a center which will seek to bond men and women of this pluralist country, to replace their fragility in their narrow spheres by the strength of civilized society bound together by a common destiny." —His Highness the Aga Khan, 49th hereditary Imam of the Ismaili Muslims, at the opening of the Ismaili Jamatkhana, in Sugar Land, Texas, 2002.

Commissioned in 2004 by IMARA Development Services to design and build a new Jamatkhana for the Plano Ismaili community, Hidell & Associates Architects designed this house of worship and community center.

FACING PAGE: Illuminated, covered walkways etched with interlocking octagons and hand-painted tiles surround a tranquil fountain, which creates a tone of calm reflection at the entry.
Photograph by Patrick Coulie

Bill Hidell brought a keen awareness of Islamic architecture gleaned from his time spent among the historic palaces, mosques and Char Baghs of captivating Isfahan, Iran. This new enduring facility infuses the transcendent qualities of Islamic architecture with modern aesthetics, facilitating cultural and social interaction in a harmonious setting.

Islamic design is predicated largely on symmetry of form and ruled by geometry. The architects selected a simple geometric pattern on which to base the facility's design—a square, rotated to arrive at interlocking octagons, the genesis for the design that permeates the facility. Set on a serene eight-acre tract in Plano, the Jamatkhana addresses the Qibla, or Mecca, while vehicular traffic is shielded outward toward the perimeter, creating an oasis of green that eschews the hurried nature of modernity.

Entering the Jamatkhana, a serene space replaces the rush of daily life. A tone of calm reflection and humility imbues the path from the front lawn up to the luminous façade of the front entry. The immaculate glass wall fronts the social lobby area—its transparency serving as an acknowledgement of this pertinent space. Always a welcoming beacon to the community, the lobby glows at night yet remains lucid during the day.

Inside the social lobby, metal panels etched with rotated squares create an evolving pattern of light and shadow onto the interlocking octagons configured in the floor. The social lobby, centrally planned as two interlocking octagons, gently orientates congregants toward the Prayer Hall. Approaching the Prayer Hall, the geometry becomes more structured, its patterns—delineated through wood, copper and stained glass on the walls, ceiling and floors—create a unity and calmness of space. Impeccably conceptualized and actualized, the

geometric motif encapsulates all ceiling, wall and lighting designs in three-dimensional form, mirroring their two-dimensional equivalents on the floor. The formal, exterior garden area, or Char Bagh, symbolizes Paradise on Earth, and is replete with a tranquil fountain and aromatic flora, which create a sublime setting for quiet contemplation or community fellowship. The Jamatkhana in Plano has fulfilled the aspirations of the Ismaili community and gives an eclectic destination to the city of Plano. ■ ■ ■ ■ ■ ■ ■ ■ ■ ■

ABOVE LEFT: The social lobby is defined by its voluminous octagonal shape, interlocking patterned floor, ornamental wood benches and lights and sculpted metal screens located on the columns.
Photograph by Patrick Coulie

ABOVE RIGHT: Metal panels etched with rotated squares create an evolving pattern of light and shadow within the interior of the social lobby.
Photograph by Patrick Coulie

FACING PAGE: Transparent glass walls signify a beacon to the community and a backdrop to the decorative, metallic screens depicting a fusion between history and contemporary.
Photograph by Patrick Coulie

Julia Yates Semmes Branch Library

■ ■

RVK Architects

■ ■ ■ ■ ■ ■ ■ ■ ■ ■ The Julia Yates Semmes Branch Library in northeast San Antonio was designed by RVK Architects to be integrated into Comanche Lookout Park, demonstrating environmental conservation techniques and providing first-rate library facilities in a captivating setting.

Set at the base of the fourth-highest point in Bexar County, the Julia Yates Semmes Branch Library is 15,975 square feet with rainwater collection, automated light-dimming and enhanced mechanical controls for reduced electrical and water usage. The existing landscape and terrain between the library and 96-acre Comanche Lookout Park vary between Texas ash juniper, mesquite, huisache and other native vegetation, while the Cibolo floodplain, a natural

ABOVE: Semmes Library, exhibited here from the northwest corner of the main entry canopy and park-side courtyard, combines environmental conservation techniques and a captivating setting to create an extraordinary public facility.
Photograph by Chris Cooper Photography

FACING PAGE: Shown from park wetlands adjacent to the library courtyard, the library uses Comanche Tower as a focal point, creating a dialog between nature and the building.
Project Design Team: Ken Rehler and Heath Wenrich.
Photograph by Chris Cooper Photography

escarpment, runs parallel to the site. The floodplain was turned into a wetlands area during an upgrade of the existing park property and was coordinated with the development of the library project to collect all parking lot surface rainwater.

The main parking area was integrated into the once-native grass field and meanders around all existing park trees. Metal cisterns located at the main entry of the building collect roof and condensate water, which is used for partial irrigation of the library landscaping. Artist-fabricated custom light bollards, wall sconces, a sitting bench and a 20-foot-tall COR-TEN sculpture relate to building and nature while drawing visitors through the building and acting as gathering nodes.

Using the Comanche Tower as a focal point, the library presents itself to the park, creating a dialogue between nature and building. This orients the main reading rooms to take advantage of park views, indirect sunlight and a seamless integration between indoor and outdoor space. This was enabled through the use of a continuous 18-foot-high glass wall along the park side of the building and a 17,000-square-foot, space frame roof structure that creates a column-free interior and dramatic overhangs ranging from eight feet to 30 feet. The glass wall and overhangs allow visitors to experience the park in any weather and create pockets of covered outdoor reading areas. On most days the 18-foot-high glass wall introduces enough light to dim the library floor lighting, while the enhanced mechanical controls

allow for precise control of the library floor, reducing electrical usage. The circulation and reference desk are positioned to give complete visual control of the library floor and operation with fewer staff. A 12-by-30-foot custom wall covering in the children's area overlays photographs of native wildflowers, rivers and live oaks with various words of recycle, renew and reuse to encourage future generations. Designed by RVK Architects, the Julia Yates Semmes Branch Library combines environmental conservation techniques and engaging site characteristics to create an exceptional public library. ■ ■ ■ ■ ■ ■ ■ ■ ■ ■

ABOVE LEFT: The interior seating areas enjoy captivating views to the courtyard and the larger outdoor environment thanks to an expansive glass exterior.
Photograph by Chris Cooper Photography

ABOVE RIGHT: Metal cisterns collect roof and condensate water, which is utilized to fulfill a portion of the library landscaping's irrigation needs.
Photograph by Chris Cooper Photography

FACING PAGE: The library courtyard is a tranquil setting combining native plantings and compelling sculpture by artist George Schroeder.
Photograph by Chris Cooper Photography

Leander Park & Ride

■ ■

McKinney York Architects

■ ■ ■ ■ ■ ■ ■ ■ ■ ■ Emanating a soft glow at twilight, the Leander Park & Ride station is abuzz with activity as commuters enjoy the subtle affability of the space during one of the day's transitional moments. Capital Metro Transportation Authority enlisted McKinney York Architects to plan, design and oversee the implementation of a new commuter and bus transfer station serving the Leander community and surrounding areas. The bustling facility on the cusp of a larger transit-oriented development—which will also serve as the terminus for Austin's forthcoming MetroRail—has been a great success, encouraging mass transit use and spurring plans for a larger transit-oriented development around the new facility.

The station has been operational since March 2007 and features 250 parking spots, a bus lane, covered drop-off and waiting areas, a clock tower and a small parkland area. Endeavoring to create a safe and welcoming station in a design indicative of a 21st-century city, illuminated supergraphics atop

FACING PAGE: Light-filled canopies provide inviting shelter during early morning and evening hours when the station is busiest.
Project Design Team: Heather McKinney, Al York and Brian Carlson.
Photograph by Greg Hursley

massive concrete piers serve as wayfinding devices—affording dusk and dawn drama while guiding patrons through the parking lot. The piers also support sheltering tensile canopies. One of the piers supports a clock tower, which affords additional wayfinding and is a branding element of Capital Metro. Safety was a top priority, and focused arteries of pedestrian traffic flow across the site to ensure efficient and safe movement of buses and people.

The canopies have luminous fabric roofs that stretch across their steel supports, expressing a light and airy quality. The dialogue between the lightweight steel and massive concrete piers creates an engaging juxtaposition. The brick used in the landscape and transit office contributes another soft material while the grids on the clock tower serve as armature for the growth of vines, introducing a third, natural element into the composition.

Sited on what had originally been farmland, a drainage requirement adjacent to the station presented design challenges but eventually was incorporated into a larger parkland encircled by walking paths, which can be used as exercise space. Located at the intersection of two new streets, this park area provides a buffer between the parking area and the streets and could be part of a future hike-and-

bike trail. A large, soft-edged detention pond was created for site drainage control and designed as an attractive landscape feature.

The recipient of a 2007 AIA Austin design award, McKinney York Architects' design and planning for the Leander Park & Ride station created a safe and appealing environment that has encouraged the community to consider its own growth in a positive light. ■ ■ ■ ■ ■ ■ ■ ■ ■ ■

ABOVE LEFT: The glowing clock tower, a part of Capital Metro's synchronized timing system, is a reassuring beacon to early morning commuters. Vines will grow up the clock tower armature, furthering the integration of manmade and natural elements.
Photograph by Greg Hursley

ABOVE RIGHT: Wayfinding graphics illuminate the surroundings and help travelers make their transit connection safely.
Photograph by Greg Hursley

FACING PAGE: Concrete, steel, fabric, brick, glass and landscaping harmoniously elevate the transit experience.
Photograph by Greg Hursley

Moises V. Vela Middle School

Gignac Associates

■ ■ ■ ■ ■ ■ ■ ■ ■ ■ The ongoing relationship between Harlingen Consolidated Independent School District and Gignac Associates has been mutually beneficial and led to the realization of several exceptional educational facilities. Completed in July 2005, Moises V. Vela Middle School was born of a shared vision resulting from that collaboration, which came to fruition on time and under budget, providing students and staff with a nurturing environment employing sustainable technologies and conveying a professional image.

Vela Middle School represents the second use of a prototype derived from a previous collaboration between Gignac Associates and HCISD that resulted in Gutierrez Middle School, albeit refinement of the prototype and distinct changes give Vela its own identity. Both projects can be characterized as non-boxy, nontraditional schools that met programmatic needs within well-defined budget parameters. Design goals associated with Vela focused on

FACING PAGE: Curvilinear elements define the entrance and drop-off areas and convey a functional and pertinent flow of traffic.
Project Design Team: Raymond Gignac, Rolando Garza, Carolyn Goldsmith-James and Juan Mujica.
Photograph by Richard Payne, FAIA

creating a professional, adult environment throughout the facility and a layout that organized academic spaces separately from more active spaces.

Isolating the gymnasium, band hall, multipurpose cafetorium and other common areas from the academic sectors, which are separated by the entrance vestibule, was of prime importance and largely drove the organization. Moreover, the radial plan provides safety and visual monitoring of student traffic, as one adult has the ability to observe three corridors from one location with minimal effort. The decision

to provide separate entrances for teachers and staff, parents and school buses helps organize traffic during peak periods, mitigating congestion. A steel structure, the school employs masonry and plaster in atypical forms, notably in the curvilinear, naturally lit cafetorium, and the color schemes, material palettes and contours create a sense of the mature for students transitioning between childhood and teenage years.

Gignac Associates has made sustainability an emphasis in all its collaborations with HCISD and this was certainly true with Vela Middle School as well. Interior daylighting is a pertinent green design feature

thanks to generous fenestration and clerestory use, and insulated skylight systems at hallway intersections break the long visual lines of the corridors. The application of high-efficiency lighting, locally and regionally derived materials and native landscaping features further augments the eco-friendly approach. Durable terrazzo floors, the patterns of which elegantly add color and design to interior spaces, are stylish and low-maintenance while the brick masonry walls do not require paint maintenance.

Meeting programmatic needs in an engaging, nontraditional facility that employs important sustainable design concepts, Gignac Associates' design of Moises V. Vela Middle School provided students and faculty with a warm, nurturing environment that assures all who enter will greet the day with aplomb. ■ ■ ■ ■ ■ ■ ■ ■ ■ ■

ABOVE LEFT: Terrazzo floors and abundant daylight are aesthetically elegant and minimize needs for maintenance and energy use.
Photograph by Richard Payne, FAIA

ABOVE RIGHT: The cafetorium affords enhanced functionality with its variety of uses.
Photograph by Richard Payne, FAIA

FACING PAGE LEFT: The entry's unique clock feature gives the corridor great interest.
Photograph by Richard Payne, FAIA

FACING PAGE RIGHT: The skylight atop the academic area helps procure a light, airy interior aura.
Photograph by Richard Payne, FAIA

Portland City Hall

■ ■

Gignac Associates

■ ■ ■ ■ ■ ■ ■ ■ ■ ■ Located on two bays affording excellent opportunities for fishing, boating, sailing, swimming and birding, the city of Portland is a quaint and charming destination on the Texas Coastal Bend. When times called for a new city hall, the mayor and city commission of Portland selected Gignac Associates to master plan and then implement a comprehensive program including new and renovated city facilities. City officials also gave Gignac Associates great latitude with the design of its new city hall, enabling the architect to create a compelling design statement within a functional and appropriate facility.

ABOVE: Curvilinear forms pay homage to nearby Corpus Christi Bay and unite with abundant glass to define Portland's atypical city hall.
Photograph by Richard Payne, FAIA

FACING PAGE: The atrium entrance is a compelling design, particularly at dusk.
Project Design Team: Raymond Gignac, Carolyn Goldsmith-James, Rolando Garza and Charles Milligan.
Photograph by Richard Payne, FAIA

Seeking to create a striking, non-traditional design with the city hall, Gignac Associates took a small-scale facility—approximately 10,000 square feet—and was able to give it presence by raising it off the ground and designing a two-story volume at the entry. A curving canopy rests atop a remarkable front entry, which is composed largely of glass, providing abundant daylighting while allowing the structure to shine in the evening. The desire to stay away from any structural forms akin to a box resulted in plentiful curves, which reflect the close proximity to Corpus Christi Bay and the water. The composition is much different than most architecture found in Portland and has been well received for its striking character.

Within the front entry, the glass atrium, reception and waiting area afford a well-lit, open space for patrons and connect to multiple suites designated for various departments. All of the offices benefit from a profusion of natural daylight. The atrium also connects upstairs to a multipurpose space that is used for meetings by the city commission as well as for municipal court purposes. Gignac Associates also designed an adjacent police station as part of the larger municipal master plan, and the two facilities share some mechanical systems. This provides energy efficiency and serves as a safeguard if one building were to experience problems related to building systems. Pre-cast materials used on the project were derived from local sources, mitigating noxious environmental effects associated with obtaining materials from far-off locations.

An atypical design for the city of Portland that met strict budget requirements for a small-scale facility yet makes a bold design statement, Giganc Associates' design and planning delivered a pristine facility that the community, city employees and visitors have been delighted with. ▪ ▪ ▪ ▪ ▪ ▪ ▪ ▪ ▪ ▪

RIGHT: Abundant transparency defines Portland City Hall.
Photograph by Richard Payne, FAIA

FACING PAGE LEFT: The curving canopy and volume of glass make a bold statement.
Photograph by Richard Payne, FAIA

FACING PAGE RIGHT: The atrium lobby benefits from generous daylighting and provides well-planned circulation and connectivity.
Photograph by Richard Payne, FAIA

St. Martin's Episcopal Church

Jackson & Ryan Architects

■ ■ ■ ■ ■ ■ ■ ■ ■ ■ As an architectural solution, St. Martin's Episcopal Church in Houston represents a deft balance of old and new. While the church embodies the imagery of a Gothic sanctuary with its towering spires, stone arches and leaded, stained glass windows, the facility also supports modern functional and acoustical needs and adhered to well-defined schedule and budget parameters. Completed within financial and scheduling requirements, Jackson & Ryan Architects' design of St. Martin's Episcopal Church enabled the congregation to build the church and parish hall of its dreams.

A defining characteristic of Gothic church architecture is its emphasis on height, both real and proportional. The nave is considerably taller than it is wide, and the corresponding relationship between its height and width falls between 2:1 and 3:1. Because the church was an infill project on the existing

FACING PAGE: Inspiration for St. Martin's Episcopal Church came from the clean lines of St. Elizabeth Church in Marburg, Germany.
Project Design Team: Guy Jackson, John Clements, Pam Camargo and Craig Pharis.
Photograph by Mark Scheyer

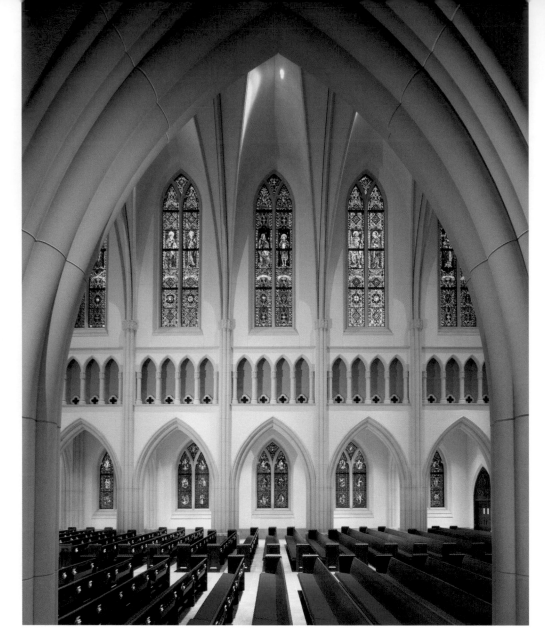

campus—combined with the desire to locate all 1,500 seats within the nave, affording unhindered views from every seat—achieving such proportions was impossible. However, Jackson & Ryan's adroit design produced the impression of immense height despite these restrictions.

Inspired by the proportions of Chartres Cathedral in France, the illusion of height was achieved in a space 55 feet wide by 70 feet high, which, albeit quite tall, does not correlate proportionally to characteristic Gothic cathedral architecture. The interior organization is long and linear with groin-vaulted ceilings and pillared arches. The pillared arches separate the side aisles, which serve as walkways, allowing all parishioners to sit in the nave and fully view the service. Increasing the height of the arched side aisles and clerestory windows above, in addition to designing a shorter triforium, further augmented the expression of verticality.

Pointed arches and thin columns direct views toward the ceiling, where copious light passes through stained glass windows, infusing the space with warmth, light and color. The interior spatial layering also emulates Chartres Cathedral, as eyes are beckoned down the nave, to the chancel and the hand-carved, quarter-sawn, white oak choir screen before culminating with the centerpiece rose window. Interior surfaces and volumes were designed to support all music and singing sans microphones—achieving authentic Gothic acoustics—while a sophisticated sound system fully hidden within the columns aids speech comprehension.

The front façade was inspired by the clean lines of St. Elizabeth Church in Marburg, Germany, and a Gothic look was achieved via uniform-colored brick, as opposed to the massive stone and hand-carved ornamentation that typically characterize Gothic architecture, which were both time- and cost-prohibitive. A pair of iconic towers with soaring spires accentuates the front entry.

The project also included the design of a new 600-seat parish hall and full banquet kitchen, nursery and educational space, a new formal cloister on the existing campus, youth center renovations and the rerouting of an adjacent thoroughfare—all of which were completed on time, allowing for continuous church operations throughout. ■ ■ ■ ■ ■ ■ ■ ■ ■ ■

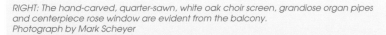

RIGHT: The hand-carved, quarter-sawn, white oak choir screen, grandiose organ pipes and centerpiece rose window are evident from the balcony.
Photograph by Mark Scheyer

FACING PAGE LEFT: Pillared arches along the nave wall separate the side aisles while immaculate stained glass above suffuses the interior with varied hues of light.
Photograph by Mark Scheyer

FACING PAGE RIGHT: The baptismal font is defined by its symmetrical lines and rich, natural materials.
Photograph by Mark Scheyer

Sunnyvale Town Hall

Ron Hobbs Architects

The town of Sunnyvale, a small community situated on the southeast edge of Lake Ray Hubbard, despite being only 20 miles east of downtown Dallas, genuinely values its rural setting and agrarian heritage. When Sunnyvale commissioned Ron Hobbs Architects in 2001 to design its first major municipal building, a new multipurpose town hall, it was essential that the new structure respect and respond to its environment and reflect the atmosphere of Sunnyvale. Completed in late 2004, Sunnyvale Town Hall captures the essence of Sunnyvale in an aesthetically appropriate, first-rate public facility, giving locals a true hub for community activities.

The town hall is situated on a wooded, sloping nine-acre site that connects via bridge to a natural 40-acre park with a lake. Tying the architecture back to nature was an emphasis, which was achieved in part through the use of stone retaining walls around the building's perimeter. The walls appear as

FACING PAGE: Sunnyvale Town Hall's offices and city council chamber sit on top of a hill and overlook the natural landscape.
Project Design Team: Ron Hobbs, Wadona Stich, Kathy Thompson, David Tobin and Michael Nagel.
Photograph by Derwin Broughton

rock ledges supporting the building and remain constant despite the ground's undulation, so the wall seemingly appears and disappears into the side of the hill depending on the terrain. Passage from the street up to the facility's parking lot intentionally follows an S-shaped path, which preserved all on-site trees and presents wonderful, changing vistas of the building as patrons drive up.

Architecturally, the structure was meant to allude to the notion of a ranch, so the massing is broken down to have the feeling of wings or multiple buildings. Texas limestone—which was also used in the retaining walls—and glass comprise the exterior palette, in addition to standing-seam metal roofs with large overhangs, which provide shade from prevailing sun angles and establish a more human scale. Intended to eschew the typical institutional feel of government buildings, the structure welcomes citizens through a front porch into a lobby that has a fireplace and many alcoves for socializing. Another feature atypical of most governmental facilities is generous fenestration in the council chamber, which connects to a back porch and terrace, affording pleasing views to a large hillside. Public corridors linked to the main lobby also serve as gallery space, and all the public spaces have multiple opportunities for usage. The public spaces and work areas are seamlessly separated from each other, with all work areas benefitting from abundant daylight, establishing a friendly and engaging work environment. For example, the council

chamber and courtroom, which have folding partitions and can be used separately or as one larger space, include expansive glazing and look out over sloping terrain.

A contextually appropriate, community-responsive architectural solution, Ron Hobbs Architects' design and planning of Sunnyvale Town Hall delivered this growing municipality a wonderful work environment and community center, reflective of the town's rural composition and love of the land. ■ ■ ■ ■ ■ ■ ■ ■ ■ ■ ■

ABOVE LEFT: Public corridors also serve as galleries to display local art and other exhibits.
Photograph by Wadona Stich

ABOVE RIGHT: The multipurpose town hall's image expresses the spirit and values of the community.
Photograph by Ron Hobbs

FACING PAGE LEFT: Stepped limestone retaining walls and native landscaping tie the building and the site together.
Photograph by Ron Hobbs

FACING PAGE RIGHT: The building's large front porches serve to welcome visitors and provide shade from the Texas sun.
Photograph by Wadona Stich

Tarrant County Subcourthouse in Arlington

LBL Architects

■ ■ ■ ■ ■ ■ ■ ■ ■ ■ Home to such popular destinations as Six Flags Over Texas, the Texas Rangers' Ballpark in Arlington, the 25,000-student-strong University of Texas at Arlington campus and the Dallas Cowboys' new state-of-the-art football stadium, a marvel of architecture and engineering ability, the city of Arlington is in the midst of exciting growth and redevelopment. This period of revitalization also includes efforts to establish a denser, more pedestrian-oriented downtown environment. As the initial architectural component of a more vibrant, walkable downtown Arlington, the new Tarrant County Subcourthouse, designed by LBL Architects, signals the beginning of grand efforts to revitalize downtown Arlington with a sustainable building of great community benefit.

Prior to the summer 2008 opening of the Tarrant County Subcourthouse, employees and patrons utilized a small facility built in 1978, which was no longer adequate for their needs. Sited on a 4.1-acre site on Abram Street in downtown Arlington, the new courthouse includes facilities for the county clerk, district

FACING PAGE: The main entrance to the new Tarrant County Subcourthouse is shown from Abram Street.
Photograph by James F. Wilson

clerk, constable, tax office, Justice of the Peace, large public meeting room and county commissioner's office. It is also one of the first structures to be designed and constructed under Arlington's new downtown design standards, which seek to promote revitalization and encourage pedestrian-friendly development. Orienting buildings close to the street, rather than being pushed back with a large parking lot in front, was one way to accomplish such a result. Establishing ample parking for a 56,000-square-foot building that receives hundreds of patrons daily was a considerable challenge. The solution was abandoning a

street to make two city blocks, pulling the building up close to the curb and then utilizing three of the four perimeter streets for parking.

Patrons of the new building enter through a prominent, centrally located rotunda, which is a three-story, glass-enclosed atrium linking the main public entrance on the west with the secondary entrance on the east. Within the rotunda, a 13-foot-wide county star adorns the terrazzo floor. The rotunda's glass, as well as the rest of the exterior's abundant glazing, is low-emissivity, allowing daylight to suffuse interiors while blocking radiant heat. High-performance glass along with cast stone, metal and brick comprise the exterior material palette. Sustainability was of great importance for Tarrant County officials, and the building is seeking LEED Silver certification. Additional green aspects include the placement of sunshades over many of the windows, heavily insulated roof and walls and highly efficient building envelope and mechanical systems, resulting in the structure being 21 percent more efficient than required by the International Energy Conservation Code. Outside the courthouse, a palette of native plant material was used for landscaping, along with a superior irrigation method known as a capillary irrigation system, which distributes water through tubes to an underground fabric that stays moist and delivers water directly to the roots. This system, employed locally in a large major facility for the first time in this area, saves precious water from being evaporated, as is the case with traditional above-ground irrigation.

The completed Tarrant County Subcourthouse has met the growing functional needs of an essential public entity, as well as its future needs—9,000 square feet of shell space allows for future growth—in an efficient structure that is leading the way in Arlington's downtown revitalization. ■ ■ ■ ■ ■ ■ ■ ■ ■ ■

TOP RIGHT: The tax collection office on the first floor features specialty license plate services.
Photograph by James F. Wilson

BOTTOM RIGHT: Justice of the Peace courtroom is one of many facilities within the Subcourthouse.
Photograph by James F. Wilson

FACING PAGE LEFT: The three-story atrium adorned with "star beams" is depicted from the west end of the Subcourthouse.
Photograph by James F. Wilson

FACING PAGE RIGHT: An interior view of the entry rotunda exhibits the "Texas Star" theme.
Photograph by James F. Wilson

Texas Association of Counties

■ ■

Steinbomer & Associates Architects

■ ■ ■ ■ ■ ■ ■ ■ ■ ■ ■ Celebrating its fourth decade serving the Lone Star State, the Texas Association of Counties is a nonprofit association that represents all 254 Texas counties' interests in the legislative process and keeps counties aware of issues that affect them. When need called for a new home for the organization, Steinbomer & Associates Architects, in a joint venture with San Antonio-based Kell-Muñoz Architects, sought to convey in the new structure materials and imagery from the two major design periods of historic Texas courthouses, which were characterized by Richardsonian and Art Deco precedents. The resultant building met TAC's programmatic needs in a stately structure evocative of Texas' greatest courthouses within a dense urban site presenting unique challenges.

ABOVE: The Texas Association of Counties building utilizes a stepped mass to transition from the low-scale neighborhood up to city-scale buildings including the State Capitol building.
Photograph by Osborne Photography

FACING PAGE: This home for county governments across Texas reflects stylistic traditions of Texas courthouses through the use of bonded brick, articulation and scaled massing elements.
Project Design Team: Robert Steinbomer, Denise Shaw of Steinbomer & Associates Architects; John Kell, Jerry Sparks and Jim Sterner of Kell-Muñoz Architects.
Photograph by Gerard D'Arcy

Located on a tight corner site at 13th and San Antonio streets, a defined edge between the Capitol complex and a historic neighborhood, the 120-foot, mid-rise structure was built to the street on two sides, an alley on one side and a property line on the other. Further complicating matters, a house on the site had been deemed historic by the Historic Landmark Commission, disallowing the removal of that property. Building around the historic home, a fully enclosed 280-car parking garage was oriented partially underground while the above-ground portion neatly wraps around the historic property.

Careful consideration was taken to break down the scale of the structure via a tripartite composition so as not to overpower smaller adjacent buildings in the neighborhood. The building's south façade fronted a series of two- and three-story buildings, so that massing was set back and scaled down such that it essentially steps down into the neighborhood. Since the north façade fronted condominiums and office towers equal in scale and height, it was able to absorb more blank mass without disrupting the neighborhood character. The incorporation of balcony setbacks overlooking downtown, a pedestrian loggia and an octagonal tower addressing the corner entry further enhanced the interaction between downtown and neighborhood.

Richardsonian and Art Deco influences are evidenced in the limestone base and rich brickwork all through the building, the turrets capping the octagonal tower and similar ventilation towers, a sloped, gable roof of slate and subtle recessing of the window panels in between the column elements. A ground-level colonnade provides additional interest and distinguishes the first-floor retail elements, above which a limestone band—which is mirrored at the top of the building—provides additional scale and character. The lower limestone banding above the colonnade features the carved names of the original 33 Texas counties and lines the periphery.

The TAC building provided the organization with offices, a boardroom and divisible 200-person capacity training center, a commercial kitchen, a law library, a full-service printing facility and a formal lobby adorned with elegant terrazzo, granite and woodwork. Fulfilling TAC's needs with a building respective of concerned neighbors, Steinbomer & Associates Architects' design recalled the greatest elements of historic Texas courthouses on a formidable site yet created a massive building with great texture and character. ■ ■ ■ ■ ■ ■ ■ ■ ■ ■

RIGHT: The tower element formally addresses the northeast corner, and the balconies on the east façade step back to reflect more traditional elements of the Capitol district. Photograph by McConnell Photography

FACING PAGE LEFT: The office tower steps away from the TAC-owned historic house and a balcony from the conference rooms has views to the Capitol. Photograph by McConnell Photography

FACING PAGE RIGHT: The executive boardroom with curved wood ceiling, wood paneling and custom conference table also features state-of-the-art teleconferencing capabilities and concealed acoustic paneling. Photograph by Osborne Photography

Texas Travel Information Center Amarillo

Richter Architects

■ ■ ■ ■ ■ ■ ■ ■ ■ ■ As the largest city in the Texas Panhandle, Amarillo has long served as both a gateway to the Lone Star State, for those entering Texas from the north, and, to a larger extent, to the American West. Its terrain is characteristic of the High Plains region; expansive flatness abounds, resulting in a land of infinite horizon. However, from this earthen pancake, undulating terrain commences and the prevailing flatness drops abruptly into dry creeks, which then lead to arroyos and on to majestic canyons. This eco-drama reaches its climax just south of Amarillo at the Palo Duro Canyon, the second-largest canyon in the United States, where years of erosion have left colorful, ribboned geologic strata that define its topography. This dramatic natural phenomenon, in which nature has truly sculpted earth, provided the inspiration for the Richter Architects-designed Texas Travel Information Center Amarillo, which articulates a regional story in both form and function.

FACING PAGE: The building emerges from the broad flatness as an earthen inversion of the nearby Palo Duro Canyon.
Project Design Team: David Richter, Elizabeth Chu Richter, Sam Morris and Stephen Cox.
Photograph by David Richter, FAIA

Located on the eastern edge of Amarillo, the Texas Travel Information Center is set on a sloping parcel near the Amarillo airport. The design called for cutting a creek into the land to serve as a functional drainage device, but also to provide an organizing element and illustrate the relationship between earth and water. As the creek traverses the site it provides a base for the building, which both cuts into the land and emerges from it. Conceptually, the design was interpreted as an earthen inversion of the canyon—rather than carving down into the terrain, the architecture emerges upward from the creek in adapted forms, which were derived from the canyon's naturalistic imagery.

Brick is the primary element of a regionally derived material palette and seven colors of brick were selected that mimic the Palo Duro Canyon's aesthetic grandeur. The design team took dirt samples from the canyon and then used computer modeling to ensure the banding and stratification were reflective of its geology. The building's forms are expressed as sculpted masses that shape the public spaces between them; weathered wood siding is detailed as a vented rain screen wall system and glazing is deeply shaded by timber-framed canopies, creating vistas through a framework of rock-like building masses. Homage is paid to the Old West through the use of gapped wood planks, which reference the region's ubiquitous wood fences and cattle chutes, and steel fabrications, which recall the art of the smith.

Conveying to visitors not only the powerful sculpture of nearby Palo Duro Canyon but a sense of the natural systems that created it, Richter Architects' design of the Texas Travel Information Center Amarillo merges land and lore, telling a story through the deft integration of purpose and art. ■ ■ ■ ■ ■ ■ ■ ■ ■

ABOVE: A drainage creek, planted with cottonwoods, natural prairie grasses and junipers, winds from the high corner of the site down to a cluster of picnic arbors.
Photograph by David Richter, FAIA

FACING PAGE LEFT: Seven brick colors carefully match the region's geologic rock strata, while weathered, planked wood and structural steel allude to the fences, barns and blacksmith craft of the West.
Photograph by Craig D. Blackmon, FAIA

FACING PAGE RIGHT: The project includes reception area, brochure and display area, multimedia room, offices, storage, 24-hour restroom facilities, picnic arbors and site development for passenger vehicles, recreational vehicles and 18-wheelers.
Photograph by Craig D. Blackmon, FAIA

CHAPTER FOUR
Industry Leaders

Gone are the days of stark white, sterile-feeling healthcare buildings and unimaginative institutional establishments. Amazing commercial complexes and research facilities showcase some of the most dazzling and innovative architecture to date.

First impressions are paramount, and architects are charged with creating an intangible feeling of awe and wonder before the actual experience even begins. Among these pages this magic is showcased in Powers Brown Architecture's Colt International headquarters, Gensler's United Way of the Texas Gulf Coast, the iconic, Rees Associates-designed Bank of America Plaza and Gideon Toal's Acme Brick Headquarters.

These industry projects are as expansive as they are high profile, and truly define the urban fabric of many cities' most prominent skylines. The talented professionals who have created the featured buildings are very conscious of this fact; it is what drives them to exceed the high expectations set forth from inception.

Hunt Consolidated Headquarters, The Beck Group, page 208

Texas State Capitol Restoration, Ford, Powell & Carson, page 220

Bank of America Plaza, Rees Associates, Inc., page 196

Acme Brick Headquarters

Gideon Toal

■ ■ ■ ■ ■ ■ ■ ■ ■ ■ One of the oldest building materials in the world, the brick has endured for centuries with its classic elegance, strength and lasting beauty. When Acme Brick, the world's largest American-owned brick company, decided to build a new corporate headquarters, it was only natural that the new structure would be comprised of brick. But the resultant design by Gideon Toal is much more than just a brick building. The 75,000-square-foot facility pays homage to brick and Acme's history in a modern structure with sustainable technologies and contemporary conveniences. Yet it is forged from traditional, lasting brick, serving as an ideal architectural solution for this venerable company to adapt and grow in the 21st century.

The November 2007 opening of the Acme Brick Headquarters along the Trinity River in Fort Worth was a major milestone for the century-plus-old corporation. Not only was it the first commercial structure built on Clearfork at Edwards Ranch, a historic property that will also include residential and mixed-use

FACING PAGE: Embracing the Trinity River, the south side of the headquarters features a covered seating area and sweeping views from the executive offices.
Photograph by Craig D. Blackmon, FAIA

development, but Acme's headquarters consolidated what had been 10-plus separate offices under one roof. Moreover, it gave employees a collaborative, far-superior work environment with new technologies and ample fenestration to take advantage of compelling river views.

Positioned along the Trinity, the site was selected for its excellent river views, its location on the Trinity Trail system and its abundance of elms, cottonwoods, ash and other mature trees. The proportions match that of the terrain so the structure does not overshadow the trees or get lost in the landscape. Parking was placed in front of the building so as not to obscure views, and existing trees were used to shade the lot and create the aura of parking spaces nestled within the trees, rather than trees placed within a parking area. Bioswales in the parking area collect and treat runoff.

The plan for an open and adaptable work environment placed private offices along the building's perimeter, which are aided by the availability of conference rooms, training facilities and a ground-floor café with terrace facing the river. A celebration of brick, the building employs creative uses of the earthen material while paying homage to the brick's history and the evolution of its production. Throughout the structure there are bricks from every one of the firm's plants; assorted Acme bricks also make up the accent walls in larger, private offices. Inside the building's elevated lobby there is a 14-foot-tall, 11-foot-wide brick mural chronicling the firm's 117-year history and its successful theme of vertical integration. Nebraska artist and stone mason Jay Tschetter also created a brick mural for the cafeteria that depicts Fort Worth's skyline and historical landmarks with the Trinity River flowing through the city.

Truly a contemporary building in function, Acme's headquarters utilizes rainwater-harvesting cisterns, proper site orientation and large roof overhangs to shade windows, LEED-friendly building materials and landscaping with minimal irrigation needs. Immensely popular with employees and locals alike, Acme Brick's new headquarters reflects the company's rich history in modern, functional forms that promote stewardship and interact harmoniously with its sylvan, riverside site. ■ ■ ■ ■ ■ ■ ■ ■ ■ ■ ■

ABOVE LEFT: Just outside the café and training center, the landscaped courtyard with pavers and seasonal plantings provides a connection to the Trinity River Trail system.
Photograph by Craig D. Blackmon, FAIA

ABOVE RIGHT: Brick pilasters define circulation corridors and give scale to otherwise long corridors in the midst of open office areas, establishing rhythm and framing Acme's celebrated art collection.
Photograph by Steven Vaughan Photography

FACING PAGE TOP: Conference rooms throughout the building are enveloped by glass walls, providing views from the circulation corridors to the river. The seating area outside this room features art made of antique equipment parts found at an Acme brick plant.
Photograph by Steven Vaughan Photography

FACING PAGE BOTTOM: Featuring a brick mural by Jay Tschetter, the employee café provides a relaxing atmosphere that seats more than 60.
Photograph by Craig D. Blackmon, FAIA

Bank of America Plaza

■ ■

Rees Associates, Inc. (formerly JPJ Architects, Inc.)

■ ■ ■ ■ ■ ■ ■ ■ ■ ■ ■ The architects of JPJ Architects—now REES—were commissioned by Bramalea, a Canadian-based developer, to design a 2-million-square-foot building that would appeal to full-floor tenants: companies demanding speedy elevator service, floorplans with usable space and excellent layout potential, more than just a handful of corner offices, unobstructed views and an aesthetically pleasing façade with landmark presence. The initial step toward meeting these objectives was devising a piggyback elevator system—the first project in the city to incorporate the technique—which significantly influenced the floor plate arrangement by reducing the elevator shaft requirements.

To ensure that the large floor plates would not make the building appear unattractively thickset, the architects devised plans for vertical loads on 16 large columns located 20 feet within the perimeter curtainwall; this creative structural solution allowed the building to be, at the time of its construction,

FACING PAGE: Just as the bank has undergone transitions in name and ownership over the years, so too has the firm that created it, keeping pace with the development of Dallas business. Bank of America Plaza's grand entry boasts a delightful interplay of geometric forms, reflectivity, translucency and light.
Project Design Team: Donald E. Jarvis, Bill Smith and Richard Flatt.
Photograph by Greg Hursley

the slenderest of its monumental height in the world. By offsetting the corners, floors average about 16 corner offices each and, sans distracting support columns, boast panoramic views. The material palette further minimizes the building's footprint and enhances its visibility. Clear glass with a hint of light silver "celebrates the street by allowing the lobby to weave itself into the fabric of the city in a welcoming gesture to passersby," relates a REES architect. Bank of America Plaza's double-paned glass, with anodized aluminum mullions, sparkles brightly during the day and glows as it reflects the sunset.

The glass itself is energy efficient, yet the architects know that people are the greatest contributors to heat gain, so they utilized a proven cooling technique by creating a system whereby the building would generate cold water during off-peak hours and then pump the chilled liquid through air conditioning coils the next day for hours of inexpensive energy.

Bank of America Plaza's design was orchestrated by the late Donald E. Jarvis, FAIA, a principal of JPJ, revered for his remarkable creativity, who alas did not see the project come to fruition—Bill Smith, FAIA, and Richard Flatt were also instrumental in its success. Thousands of people enjoy it daily, arriving at the adjacent double-helix parking structure, traveling through underground pedestrian passageways and rising to their destinations in elevators adorned with interchangeable, custom-woven tapestries that echo the structure's artful quality. The building has had a profound revitalizing effect on Dallas' historic West End and stands today as timeless as when it was conceived. ■ ■ ■ ■ ■ ■ ■ ■ ■ ■

ABOVE LEFT: An artful architectural design and clever structural engineering allow more than a dozen corner offices on each level to have unobstructed views of the city.
Photograph by Greg Hursley

ABOVE RIGHT: The brightly hued sculpture punctuates the powerful presence of the building, which is evident from every vantage—especially looking skyward from the base.
Photograph by Greg Hursley

FACING PAGE: Erected in 1984, the 72-story building glimmers at night, with its signature, sculptural character eloquently expressed in the unique argon tube lighting.
Photograph by Greg Hursley

Colt International

■ ■

Powers Brown Architecture

■ ■ ■ ■ ■ ■ ■ ■ ■ ■ For years industrial buildings were built via inexpensive and efficient yet homogenous tilt-wall construction that led to the concept of "big dumb boxes." Eschewing this hackneyed, economics-first approach, Powers Brown Architecture has designed many small smart boxes for business owners who are more aware of architecture and desire to have a pleasing work environment that meets their employees' needs. The owners of Colt International were two such business owners who wanted a more responsive solution that also fit their budget. The firm's headquarters as designed by Powers Brown Architecture responds to the firm's organization in a compelling structure with great character.

ABOVE: Designed to meet specific organizational needs and provide employees with an outstanding work environment, the architecture is a refutation of the "big dumb box" ideology employed in so many industrial buildings.
Photograph by Geoffrey Lyon

FACING PAGE: The illuminated canvas awning is distorted to evoke the skin/frame of early planes—an interest of both the owners.
Project Design Team: Jeffrey Brown, Nazir Khalfe, John Cadenhead and Megan Ebert.
Photograph by Geoffrey Lyon

Colt International is a fast-growing firm that essentially facilitates executive air travel on private jets across borders and nationally. After outgrowing its start-up office space, the company purchased an economical infill site set in an older office park located between downtown Houston and the Gulf of Mexico in Webster. The organization of the 22,248-square-foot headquarters directly relates to the firm's functional endeavors. Each Colt owner emphasizes a particular business aspect: one supervises the area of the business that monitors flights—plans, tracks and routes each plane's progress—while the other commands the firm's general support, which includes fuel purchase agreements, applications for permission to land and passport and visa issues.

Two rooms housing the collective aspects of both of these programs are formed by an S-shaped bar that affords general support, and each room is sized based upon its intended function and number of employees and lit to serve those functions. The office park is situated in a coastal plain with conifer trees so both rooms benefit from the appropriate exterior views. Each view is accompanied by an oversized picture window, which is screened by a canvas awning that has been distorted to evoke the skin and frame of early planes—an interest shared by both owners. The canvas awnings also serve to create an outside, interstitial porch landscape for employee use.

The configuration of spaces enables several pertinent circulation routes to occur within the structure, the most important of which is the prospective client tour. From the lobby visitors walk through a small passage to the conference room and then out to an elevated dais overlooking the assortment of flight-monitor screens in the smaller of the two rooms. Other routes in the facility provide for direct interface between the two distinct functions; a series of cut-throughs allows employees to bypass the two, enabling quick coordination of a route in progress and enhanced efficiency.

Powers Brown Architecture's design for Colt International met functional needs within budget parameters and illustrates that industrial buildings can be both functional and have great architectural character. ■ ■ ■ ■ ■ ■ ■ ■ ■ ■

RIGHT: A compelling interplay of light characterizes the patio area with picture windows screened by the canvas awning.
Photograph by Geoffrey Lyon

FACING PAGE LEFT: Like many spaces within, the porcelain tile hall facing the patio receives generous interior daylighting.
Photograph by Geoffrey Lyon

FACING PAGE RIGHT: The reception area's welcoming aesthetic is enhanced with birch veneer trim.
Photograph by Geoffrey Lyon

Doctors Hospital at Renaissance

The Warren Group Architects, Inc.

For many years the people of the Rio Grande Valley lacked opportunities for premier patient care at local medical facilities. Healthcare treatments requiring the latest medical technologies typically meant a considerable trip to Houston. As a physician-owned medical center serving a rapidly growing population, Doctors Hospital at Renaissance in Edinburg has grown steadily from its inception as an outpatient surgical center in 1997 into a full-service hospital with an array of pertinent facilities—each of which reflects this diverse medical community's earnest commitment to providing the highest-quality patient care.

Principal Laura Nassri Warren, AIA, of The Warren Group Architects made providing a first-class, dignified healing environment her top priority, which meant designing with patients in mind and being respective of what they endure. Laura had been appalled at some of the conditions she witnessed

FACING PAGE: The pediatric courtyard at Renaissance Behavioral Hospital faces an expansive wall of glass, blurring the line between interior and exterior.
Photograph by Daniel Aguilar

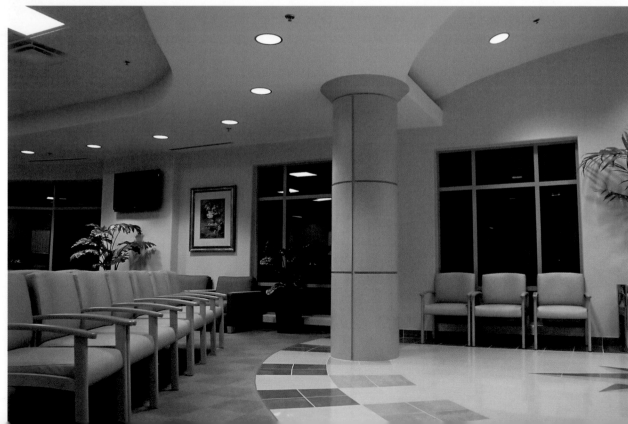

at other facilities: individuals dropped off in stretchers to cramped, common waiting areas and the general inadequacy of accommodations. In addition to collaborating closely with nurses, technicians and specialists of the hospital, she took her design team to different facilities in the area to observe firsthand the plight of the patient.

A full-service hospital, Doctors Hospital at Renaissance includes a 45,000-square-foot, three-story oncology center, a 200,000-square-foot women's hospital, an 80-bed behavioral hospital—which is subdivided into geriatric, adult, adolescent and pediatric centers—and a 320-bed general hospital facility, which houses nuclear medicine, general surgery, heart center, diagnostic centers and labs. Reflective of the local vernacular, the architecture employs a regional and Mediterranean style with stucco, clay tile and heavy trim. Throughout the project the value and healing potential of color was emphasized greatly; a color study at the onset evidenced the value of warm, soothing tones as well as the potential of more active colors like green, which encourages achievement. For example, the waiting room includes a dome painted with blue hues so that light reflects down and provides a light of hope to patients. The blue is picked up in the carpet and complemented by healing earth tones. Along with color, natural light is of paramount importance, and all non-radiation areas enjoy abundant daylighting.

The nurses' desires were for efficiency, adaptability and minimizing the patient wait. A secondary waiting area was implemented and the nurses' working environments were enhanced. Dependent on each nurse's role, nurse stations are centered in each wing and highly specialized based on function and relationships with others so every process has a constant flow. The waiting

areas have a living room setting, enlivened with color, televisions, comfortable chairs and certain spaces designed for interaction, which invite families or fellow patients to be a part of the healing process.

A healing environment of dignity rooted in the patient experience, Doctors Hospital at Renaissance is the non-institutional, technologically superior medical center the people of the Rio Grande Valley had long hoped for. ■ ■ ■ ■ ■ ■ ■ ■ ■ ■

ABOVE LEFT: A recessed ceiling element in the cancer center's waiting room and reception area affords great character and interest, eschewing the institutional feel typically associated with healthcare facilities.
Photograph by Daniel Aguilar

ABOVE RIGHT: Mediterranean-inspired details found throughout the campus are reflective of the regional architectural vernacular that is common throughout the Rio Grande Valley.
Photograph by Daniel Aguilar

FACING PAGE TOP: Awash with vibrant and soothing colors, the pediatric day room is an engaging, restorative environment.
Photograph by Daniel Aguilar

FACING PAGE BOTTOM: The family waiting area/lobby was envisioned as a living room-style setting where interaction between families and fellow patients aids the healing process.
Photograph by Daniel Aguilar

Hunt Consolidated Headquarters
The Beck Group

■ ■ ■ ■ ■ ■ ■ ■ ■ ■ From its prominent setting in the Dallas Arts District, neighboring such architectural gems as the Dallas Museum of Art and the Nasher Sculpture Center, Hunt Consolidated Headquarters might easily be mistaken for another repository of fine art. The façade fronting heavily trafficked Woodall Rodgers Freeway employs a striking, curved wall of glass—which is intersected by a vertical glass ellipse at both the base and top of the curvilinear plane—making a dynamic statement at the entrance to downtown along its northern edge. Designed by The Beck Group after winning a competition among other national firms, Hunt Consolidated Headquarters gives great prominence to this world leader among independent energy companies, affording class-A office space for employees while enhancing the rich urban fabric of downtown Dallas.

FACING PAGE: The building's north façade fronting Woodall Rodgers Freeway is a dynamic, curved wall of glass with vertical ellipses at the base and top of the plane.
Project Design Team: Rick del Monte, Hoyt Hammer, Brian Miller, Ed McGonigle and Jason Aboujeib.
Photograph by Charles Davis Smith, AIA

Set at the prominent intersection of Woodall Rodgers and Akard Street, the structure was envisioned as a gateway into downtown. The presence of the historic Cumberland Hill School—built in 1889, it is the city's only remaining 19th-century school building—across the street called for architecture respectful of its historic fabric. Thus, the 14-story structure was sited as far east on the property as possible to not overpower the historic property. Moreover, the façade facing the school was planned as a curve spanning almost two full blocks, which created a nice urban space across the street from the school. Since the school is surrounded by large live oaks, this outdoor pocket was designed to create a mirroring green space and, in its larger context, a green gateway into downtown.

The base of the 475,000-square-foot building is comprised of yellowish Texas limestone, which reflects the color of the adjacent Cumberland School, while the top of the building features Brazilian granite; the palette reflects the general color and tone of the Arts District, from the gray limestone on the DMA and limestone in the Meyerson Symphony Center to the warm, yellowy travertine in the Nasher. The walls were treated like a skin, with full-height glass on the exterior slicing and folding as it traverses the building, emphasizing the edges of the various planes. The high-performance, low-reflectance glass includes special shading on the backside, and the glass is broken into three panels, the upper and lower of which have a ceramic frit painted on to block a large portion of heat coming into the building. The building is slated to receive LEED certification for commercial interiors.

Providing Hunt Consolidated with a first-rate structure that is mindful of the Dallas Arts District's grand architectural character, the headquarters as designed by The Beck Group established a gateway into downtown Dallas via an iconic structure that has enriched the Dallas skyline. ■ ■ ■ ■ ■ ■ ■ ■ ■ ■ ■ ■

ABOVE: The curving west façade, comprised of both tower and parking garage, creates an urban pocket respective of the adjacent Cumberland School, a historic property.
Photograph by Charles Davis Smith, AIA

RIGHT: A fountain at the base of the tower, along with live oak trees and landscaping, lends itself to a tranquil exterior ambience on the ground level.
Photograph by Charles Davis Smith, AIA

FACING PAGE: The Hunt Consolidated Headquarters is a striking component of downtown Dallas' picturesque skyline.
Photograph by Charles Davis Smith, AIA

Market Street – The Woodlands

■ ■

TBG Partners

■ ■ ■ ■ ■ ■ ■ ■ ■ ■ The 2004 completion of Market Street at The Woodlands gave Houston's suburban neighbor to the north a vibrant city center and must-visit destination. An eclectic mix of restaurants and retail offerings, Market Street combines an array of architectural styles with vibrant, activated landscapes and streetscapes that capture the essence of small-town, mid-century Texas. Skillfully planned and designed by TBG Partners, this buoyant outdoor environment predicated on simultaneously distinct and integrated zones has given The Woodlands a community hub that goes far beyond shopping.

The stylistic approach for Market Street was derived from nostalgia for small-town Texas. Just as a small town frequently has new structures built next to older buildings, the architecture within Market Street echoes this mosaic arrangement, resulting in a heterogeneous mixture of façades and vernaculars.

FACING PAGE: A dynamic hub at the heart of The Woodlands, Market Street is a pedestrian-oriented environment emphasizing connectivity and urbanity within a small-town atmosphere.
Photograph by Walter Larrimore

Heeding this configuration, TBG Partners designed streetscapes, landscaping and outdoor environments that pertain to particular eras and are reflective of their proximate architecture.

Visitors to Market Street enter into an area known as restaurant row, which has a dense urban feel with a fairly small street section, ample pedestrian sidewalks and low stone walls that guide patrons through the area. Market Street is organized to navigate patrons through its various uses, creating a distinct sense of place that encourages interaction with the landscape. Passage through restaurant row gives way to a common lawn area known as Central Park. Depressed from curb level, this oval-shaped, multifunctional space becomes Market Street's unifying focal point while providing a perimeter for hosting activities. A mature live oak anchors the east end and serves as that one prominent tree found in most small-town parks. Within this green space, an elevated, interactive fountain with LED lights and constantly changing volumes of water is an immensely popular feature. The fountain can also be turned off to double as a stage for Market Street's weekly spring and summer concerts.

TOP LEFT: Enjoying the benefits of Market Street's small-town configuration, visitors stroll down sidewalks that use street trees as a vegetative buffer separating retail from parking areas.
Photograph by TBG Partners

BOTTOM LEFT: Children play in Central Park's choreographed fountain surrounded by planters and native and adaptive plants indicative of those that appear throughout Market Street.
Photograph by TBG Partners

FACING PAGE LEFT: Narrow, pedestrian-friendly streets link retail throughout the site, promoting connectivity and community interaction while reinforcing Market Street's small-town character.
Photograph by Walter Larrimore

FACING PAGE RIGHT: Festival lighting, street trees and plantings adorn activated streetscapes that link architectural styles ranging from Depression-era to post-war design expressions, creating a dynamic experience.
Photograph by TBG Partners

West of Central Park are several coffee and juice stores, between which an alley known as "the mews" provides a passive, stone plaza seating area with ample tables and chairs, potted plants and a tranquil wall fountain. Active streetscapes also change through various zones, as parallel parking gives way to front-end parking and 1960s-styled parking meters. The parking meters are not obligatory, but are functioning and all proceeds go to charity.

Carefully combining active and passive zones in a wholly engaging civic center, TBG's planning and design for Market Street has given The Woodlands a robust destination in which patrons uncover new experiences upon every visit. ■ ■ ■ ■ ■ ■ ■ ■ ■ ■ ■

McAllen Convention Center

■ ■

Gignac Associates

■ ■ ■ ■ ■ ■ ■ ■ ■ ■ ■ As part of a larger master plan effort creating an engaging retail and entertainment district, McAllen city officials commissioned Gignac Associates, in collaboration with Atlanta-based TVS, to create a new convention center that would serve as the centerpiece. Completed in April 2007, the $50 million project included the master-planned district and new convention center along with administrative offices, site amenities and landscaping and was completed within one percent of the original budget estimate. Gignac Associates' wealth of large-scale project experience, particularly convention and conference centers, proved invaluable in meeting the goals set forth by McAllen city officials.

ABOVE: The McAllen Convention Center reflects regional architecture and is the centerpiece of a vibrant new entertainment and retail district.
Photograph by Brian Gassel, TVS

FACING PAGE: The grand entrance, clock tower and arcade of the McAllen Convention Center are compelling and stately against the night sky.
Project Design Team: Raymond Gignac, Robert Svedberg, Jack Plaxco and John Cutler.
Photograph by Brian Gassel, TVS

The design team worked closely with McAllen city officials, who wanted to make a statement about regional architecture, creating a convention center reflective of south Texas' cultural influences while maintaining a modern appreciation for light and space. Being in such close proximity to the Mexican border—the convention center is literally 15 minutes away from America's southern neighbor—ubiquitous Spanish, Mexican and Southwestern influences can be found throughout McAllen and were thus reflected in the new convention center via masonry structures capped with red-tile roofs. Working within that regional Southwest vernacular, the architect met modern desires for large, open spaces filled with light, which are evidenced in the main convention center building's large wall of glass on the front exterior. An expansive pane of glass affords daylighting and generous views, while an additional layer of fritted glass

and an entrance canopy above cut down on glare. The convention center abuts a stately clock tower, which is intended to serve as a wayfinding device and a beacon for the facility.

Sited on an undeveloped, 100-acre tract of land, another design goal was to skillfully blur the line between interior and exterior. Ample fenestration obviously brings views and lush landscape elements inside, and generous outdoor spaces are adorned with fountains, reflecting pools, a bandstand and other outdoor amenities. Architectural design elements further enhance interior-exterior continuity, such as a winding interior corridor with arched doorways that is brought outside as an arched walkway that will likely tie into future facilities, perhaps a performing arts center.

Creating a large-scale master plan and centerpiece convention center in structural forms evocative of

McAllen's rich heritage—albeit with contemporary expressions devoid of such regional architecture—

Gignac Associates collaborated with TVS and McAllen city officials to procure an ideal architectural

solution that will be admired for generations. ■ ■ ■ ■ ■ ■ ■ ■ ■

ABOVE LEFT: The elegant ballroom includes a custom-designed light fixture above the Axminster carpet.
Photograph by Brian Gassel, TVS

ABOVE RIGHT: An exterior palm court with tranquil fountain is an ideal space for outdoor respite.
Photograph by Brian Gassel, TVS

FACING PAGE LEFT: The exterior structural glass is a delicate balance of engaging aesthetics and energy-efficient functionality.
Photograph by Brian Gassel, TVS

FACING PAGE RIGHT: The interior arcade design element extends outside, blurring the line between interior and exterior.
Photograph by Brian Gassel, TVS

Texas State Capitol Restoration

■■■■■■■■■■■■■■■■■■■■■■■■■■■■■■■■■■

Ford, Powell & Carson

■ ■ ■ ■ ■ ■ ■ ■ ■ ■ ■ Taller than the U.S. Capitol, the Texas State Capitol is a grand structure befitting of a grand state. Architecturally, the Capitol is renowned for its Renaissance Revival style formed from Texas granite, and is one of AIA's top 100 buildings from its 2007 "America's Favorite Architecture" poll commemorating the organization's 150th anniversary. Originally completed in 1888, the Capitol required significant restorations by 1988, when Ford Powell & Carson began work on a massive restoration project that spanned more than seven years. Restoring the Capitol to its formerly pristine condition, the project team was mindful of its original structural intent while meeting modern, significantly expanded functional needs and preserving views to the Capitol from all vantages.

FACING PAGE: The Texas Capitol's ceremonial entry facing South Congress exhibits the sheet metal and cast-iron dome, copper standing-seam roof and handsome Texas pink granite. Photograph by Greg Hursley

At the time of the restoration, the Capitol encompassed more than 370,000 square feet yet required an additional extension of 300,000 square feet plus ample parking space to meet growing legislative needs. The challenge of doubling the existing square footage without disturbing views was solved by burrowing through thick limestone—which required skilled engineering not to harm the existing foundation—and extending the Capitol underground. New House and Senate offices were placed underground along an internal atrium courtyard that picks up Congress Avenue's north-south axis. Elevators on either end lead to street-level pavilions, enabling patrons to pass between Capitol and underground within moments. In addition to infusing the underground extension with light, the sky-lit corridor's positioning allows people to peer up and view the Capitol's dome through the skylight. The extension was primarily the work of joint venture partner 3D/I.

Large rooms and open areas of the historic Capitol had subsequently been reduced to a rabbit warren of small spaces, mostly without windows for natural daylight. In the restoration, larger areas were subdivided with glass above the door lines, which exhibited how the room was originally scaled while providing naturally lit, smaller spaces and new functions. Because the original structure lacked air conditioning, multiple renovations over the years had resulted in ubiquitous ad hoc installations, and original spaces and superb architectural elements were frequently decimated by exposed ductwork. Removing these eyesores helped reestablish the robust spaces and architectural features from years past; the interior was cleaned, repainted and scraped down where needed and carefully restored in its entirety.

The Capitol's granite exterior held up remarkably well over the years, so the mortars were repaired and remnants of black mortar detected in all the joints were put back. The roof leaks in specific areas were repaired, and the skylights

over the House and Senate chambers were restored. On the dome, paint was stripped down and new coatings were applied. The approximately 800 12-foot-tall windows on the exterior were restored on an individual basis, each of which was in varying degrees of deterioration. The original cherry wood shutters were replicated and replaced, giving the structure additional scale and unity.

In sum, Ford Powell & Carson's deft planning and design restored the Texas Capitol to impeccable condition while retaining its historic character and meeting modern functional requirements. ■ ■ ■ ■ ■ ■ ■ ■ ■ ■ ■

ABOVE LEFT: The skin of the dome's cavernous interior is restored sheet metal that was repainted with decorative gold trim.
Photograph by Greg Hursley

ABOVE RIGHT: The restored sheet metal and cast-iron dome was stripped, repaired and repainted in this historic pink color to match the building's granite façades.
Photograph by Greg Hursley

FACING PAGE: Restored oak woodwork, cast-iron railings, sheet metal and plaster balcony ornamentation exude elegance in the extraordinary rotunda.
Photograph by Greg Hursley

United Way of the Texas Gulf Coast

Gensler

■ ■ ■ ■ ■ ■ ■ ■ ■ ■ A laudable organization long dedicated to mobilizing the caring power of communities, the United Way of the Texas Gulf Coast, an entity reliant on the benevolent acts of local individual and corporate citizens, epitomizes the type of organization that depends on a strong community presence for its resources. For years the United Way lacked such a presence, officing from several floors of a nondescript office building just off the 610 Loop. Providing the United Way with an extraordinary civic identity in spaces fostering a collaborative approach, Gensler helped United Way achieve its goals in flexible and functional yet striking architectural forms.

Through the design of its new headquarters the United Way of the Texas Gulf Coast sought to grow its annual campaign, provide employees and users a great work environment and achieve a greater presence in the community. The desire for increased visibility was achieved literally and figuratively through

FACING PAGE: Scaled to blend with the townhomes in the area, the United Way of the Texas Gulf Coast expresses the two-story campaign halls and the articulated roofline. Photograph by Joe Aker, Aker/Zvonkovic Photography

an expansive glass façade, which invites views into the facility and affords sweeping vistas out to Houston's central core; it also reflects the organization's emphasis on being open to the community. Built as a tilt-up structure, the walls were clad in brick, which was complemented by a palette of high-performance glass and cast stone. Lending the architecture great interest and character, compelling roof elements atop

each of the glass forms were raised on the north side to permit sunlight and lowered on the south end and aided by deep overhangs to control the sun. Astute building orientation was augmented by the use of insulated, high-performance glass, interior shading devices, overhangs and a layer of fritted glass to control glare and solar heat gain.

Comprising approximately 90,000 square feet, the United Way features approximately 65,000 square feet of administrative space, a 25,000-square-foot community resource center and a 400-plus-car parking garage. The administrative portion is organized around four campaign halls, which are flexible, two-story spaces that helped organize and modulate the building. The Jesse H. Jones Community Resource Center is organized around a large pre-function space that is flexible and well lit. Surrounded by meeting rooms, the CRC includes a computer learning center and a ballroom-sized meeting area that can be subdivided into six smaller rooms. An engaging outdoor space between the administrative building and the CRC, which is bounded by the building on three sides and adorned with large trees and a garden, is a wonderful green space for events or leisure.

A cost-effective yet compelling and adaptable architectural solution, the United Way of the Texas Gulf Coast headquarters as planned and designed by Gensler gave the organization a vibrant identity in central Houston that has greatly enhanced the efficacy of its altruistic mission and investment in the community. ■ ■ ■ ■ ■ ■ ■ ■ ■ ■

CHAPTER FIVE
Sustaining Growth

The natural environment is affected by a variety of everyday decisions—and this certainly includes where, how and with what materials buildings are constructed. A city's built environment is a remarkably significant contributor to its carbon footprint; in fact, according to most estimates buildings account for nearly half of all greenhouse gas emissions. As a result, today's architects are making a genuine and laudable commitment to protecting our natural environment through the design and construction of energy-efficient, responsible architectural solutions.

The efforts of building design aimed at ensuring a more positive outlook for the future are evident in projects from Graeber, Simmons & Cowan's design for AMD's corporate campus to BNIM Architects' Fayez S. Sarofim Research Building. The tenets, ideas and revelations of sustainability are nothing new: Our planet is affected by the way we live. However, the commitment to green building practices has grown and evolved into tangible methods, which architects are increasingly incorporating into their projects. From renewable materials to energy-conserving electrical resources—these architects are discovering new innovations that are changing architecture's impact on our world. It is a passionate topic, but this passion for discovering and incorporating renewable resources has brought green design and building to the forefront.

That these practices will soon become commonplace in all forms of construction is the hope of many architects. Beneficial techniques that were once thought impossible are now not only possible but affordable as well. The professionals who employ these commendable methods are eloquently leading the way for others to follow.

World Birding Center, Lake I Flato Architects, page 266

Kelly Lane Middle School, SHW Group - Austin, page 246

AMD

Graeber, Simmons & Cowan

■ ■ ■ ■ ■ ■ ■ ■ ■ ■ When the global technology company AMD decided in 2004 to build a new corporate campus to consolidate its Austin-based design and administrative functions, it selected Graeber, Simmons & Cowan to program, plan and design its campus site, buildings and interiors. Seeking to capture the essence of the Hill Country in progressive forms befitting of a leading technology company, the design reflects a deep commitment to sustainability while providing AMD with an exceptional workplace benefiting both employees and the environment.

The original development plan sought to expediently solve AMD's space and consolidation needs via build-to-suit office buildings on the developer's land. After several months AMD decided instead to purchase land and create an AMD-specific campus, changing not just the opportunities but the vision as well. The site selected, a 59-acre hilltop parcel, is a unique setting, central with respect to the employee base. Located in southwest Austin,

FACING PAGE: A collection of forms along a central gallery housing corporate services, the commons building was sited carefully between the stepped savanna and the dry woodlands protected areas.
Project Design Team: Tom Cornelius, Katheryn Lott, Ed Richburg, Bonny Gray, Julie Zitter, Greg Aranda and Vivian Price.
Photograph by Barton Wilder Custom Images

the site was recognized as an environmentally sensitive geographical area. Thus the commitment was made to develop the campus in a way that would minimize imminent construction impact and respond to long-term energy and environmental criteria, which became the driving force behind the design.

Designed as a series of inward-facing, interconnected buildings, the campus was envisioned as a first-rate design center that would be a successful recruiting tool both in and out of Austin—the city is home to many microprocessor design companies. A compelling design statement is the inverted roof form that is replicated in buildings throughout the campus. The visually striking roof articulates the rainwater collection system, which is an integral component of the campus' intention to achieve LEED Gold certification.

Rainwater is collected from all the roof surfaces, including the garages; the storage capacity is approximately 1.5 million gallons. The water reserve is partitioned so that 400,000 gallons of the aggregate amount will be used for irrigation purposes. While a palette of hearty, native plant material was selected, irrigation assures flowers and grasses thrive and bloom; irrigation needs will be fulfilled entirely from rainwater harvesting. The remainder of the harvested rainwater will be used by the cooling towers, supplying about 15 percent of those annual water needs. Aside from the reduction in potable water needs, the rooftop rain collection never becomes runoff and thus does not require conventional stormwater treatment.

Graeber, Simmons & Cowan's design and planning for AMD's corporate campus reflects a sincere pledge to sustainability in a setting that reflects the client's forward thinking and commitment to its workforce. ■ ■ ■ ■ ■ ■ ■ ■ ■ ■ ■

ABOVE: Pedestrian bridges span roadways and undisturbed areas, providing level access that connects the east campus buildings to the centrally located commons building.
Photograph by Barton Wilder Custom Images

RIGHT: A 20,000-gallon central cistern is the collection point for rainwater spilling from the commons building's rooftops.
Photograph by Atelier Wong Photography

FACING PAGE TOP: The employee lobby, a secure point to all office areas, research spaces and to the exterior courtyards, is situated opposite the building entrance.
Photograph by Atelier Wong Photography

FACING PAGE BOTTOM: Covered walkways are used as gathering points and define the pedestrian arcades, which are featured in all office buildings and parking garages.
Photograph by Atelier Wong Photography

Arbor Hills Nature Preserve

■ ■

MESA

■ ■ ■ ■ ■ ■ ■ ■ ■ ■ Plano's 200-acre gem of a parcel with an 80-foot change in topographic elevation was originally planned as a sports complex, but MESA instantly saw its raw beauty and potential and proposed alternate plans to city officials, including liaison Kenneth Phelps, who fully appreciated and believed in MESA's vision. Arbor Hills is a microcosm of what north Texas looked like before it was settled—blackland prairie, riparian forest and upland forest areas. The rarity of these three diverse ecosystems coexisting so closely and surviving the area's rigorous development heightened the importance of restoring the land so that it could serve as both a teaching tool and a place for recreation.

The trails of Arbor Hills Nature Preserve are gently woven into the natural topography, ensuring minimal impact on the ecosystem and providing fresh panoramas around every bend. Arbor Hills is best described as a series of experiences, not only while enjoying the meandering trails and vistas but also

FACING PAGE: Created in phase two, the Sentinel Tower overlooks the grandeur of the park.
Project Design Team: Stan Cowan, Robin McCaffrey, Mike Fraze and Fred Walters.
Photograph by Tom Jenkins

from the moment visitors turn north from Parker Road and make their way through the curvilinear parking. Its spiraling form mimics the manner in which a tornado would move across the terrain, a metaphor for man's destructive influence on the land. At the core of the parking facility, a bioswale, which collects rainwater from the sloped concrete surface and naturally filters the storm-water runoff before it recharges the groundwater table, has proven a point of intrigue for adults and children alike.

Though a portion of the land was beyond restoration due to decades of agrarian use, MESA approached the seeming negative as an opportunity to be creative. The firm's professionals utilized the space for built elements like the parking facility, farmstead-inspired picnic shelters and silo-shaped bathrooms, giving a distinctive agrarian flavor to the design of each and even nostalgically preserving the windmill-capped cistern. To restore the blackland prairie to its original state, a grassland burn was instituted, decimating invasive plant life and allowing seeds of native species to regerminate. With its strong oaks and elms and under-story of mixed shrubbery, the upland forest required little editing other than the removal of a few species of nonnative trees with excessive hydration needs. As the interpretive signage communicates, it takes dangerously little to upset nature's delicate balance.

MESA, along with Larson Pedigo Architects, conceived of the master plan and successfully brought the first phase to life by approaching nature with humility, every step of the way. Benches sit low to the ground, allowing tall grasses to quietly envelop visitors; trails do not inconvenience the land's myriad wildlife; and the lookout tower—despite man's innate inclination to place it as the center of attention atop a hill—is perched only halfway from the base of the upland forest's slope, unobtrusively fostering panoramic views. A rarity in projects of this

nature, several years after the first phase was finished, the city of Plano acquired more than 100 acres of land—as specified in the master plan—and MESA was able to fulfill the original vision in its entirety. The Burr Oak Pavilion is now complemented by the more-recently erected Sentinel Tower, creating an architectural dialogue across the park. A hallmark of MESA's portfolio, Arbor Hills was the earliest park of its kind in the area and, at the time of its development, one of only a few in the country. Its warm reception inspired other cities to attempt to follow suit. ■ ■ ■ ■ ■ ■ ■ ■ ■ ■

ABOVE LEFT: The main trail bridge at Indian Creek leads to numerous panoramic vistas. Every visitable area of the preserve is enjoyed via accessible paths.
Photograph by Tom Jenkins

ABOVE RIGHT: Adjacent to the pavilion complex is the granary-inspired restroom facility, which was designed by Larson Pedigo Architects.
Photograph by Charles Smith

FACING PAGE: Looking to the south, the Sentinel Tower and the sky bridge that leads up to it overlook the Indian Creek tributary.
Photograph by Tom Jenkins

Dell Children's Medical Center of Central Texas

TBG Partners

■ ■ ■ ■ ■ ■ ■ ■ ■ ■ Dell Children's Medical Center of Central Texas is a state-of-the-art children's hospital that is creating a new standard in pediatric care. The world's first hospital to seek LEED Platinum certification, this world-class medical center is a comprehensive healing environment predicated on the principles of sustainable design. TBG Partners created a design for this innovative new facility that provides vibrant spaces for patients to rejuvenate and reconnect with nature within the confines of the hospital.

Emphasizing the curative powers of the natural environment, interior and exterior landscapes revitalize patients, multisensory stimuli foster recovery and windows throughout the hospital open to therapeutic views of nature. A three-acre signature healing garden is defined by textured and brightly colored surfaces that provide significant therapeutic benefits. Entry to this garden is marked by a 30-inch granite sphere, slightly elevated by water and held within

FACING PAGE: Characterized by vibrant colors and energized forms, the healing garden incorporates various elements that engender therapy, engaging patients in the active experience of triumph.
Photograph by John Durant

a granite cradle. This floating stone fountain allows patients to safely spin a two-ton granite ball with ease, engendering a therapeutic feeling of triumph that an object so massive can easily be moved by a child. TBG's design called for a variety of passive and active spaces harmoniously stitched together across an eclectic environment. Some favorite design elements include a colorful peek-a-boo wall with circular windows at varying heights, which is used as a maze by children of all ages, a human sundial plaza that allows patients to use their own shadows to show time, a multimedia movie plaza, a meditative labyrinth and a butterfly garden.

Reflecting the biodiversity of central Texas, TBG's design includes six courtyard environments that represent the six eco-regions comprised by the 46 counties served by Dell Children's. From Texas' arid rolling plains to the coastal climates of the south, distinctive courtyards characterize each region, integrating the

sub-tropical plantings with central Texas pines. Perhaps the most prominent feature within the central courtyard, a three-story waterway cascades down a granite wall into a serpentine stream then flows over a rock waterfall into a serene reflecting pool. These water features create aural tranquility for patients, families and healthcare workers who benefit from engagement with the sound of flowing water.

Proof of a truly green project in both design and construction, the reclaimed water irrigation system significantly minimizes the hospital's need for potable water while 30,000 square feet of courtyards illuminate the hospital's interior, reducing daytime lighting and energy consumption. Resilient, regionally appropriate native and adaptive plants utilize underground drip irrigation to further alleviate water needs. Recycled content was used liberally, including composite wood, recycled glass and high fly-ash content concrete, and all woods were FSC-certified. Several interior courtyards feature green roofs, which were installed for

thermal value and to reinsert habitat inside the building footprint. A brilliant model of sustainability, TBG Partners' design for Dell Children's Medical Center of Central Texas provides healing environments that are an essential component of this pioneering facility in pediatric care. ■ ■ ■ ■ ■ ■ ■ ■ ■ ■ ■

ABOVE: Concrete with high fly-ash content was sculpted over wire mesh to create the rock waterfall at the base of the central courtyard's expansive water feature.
Photograph by TBG Partners

RIGHT: Dell Children's main entrance prefigures the landscape design's emphasis on color and light in spaces reserved for therapy and active play.
Photograph by John Durant

FACING PAGE: Designed for active play, the healing garden's peek-a-boo wall is a vibrantly painted maze articulated by dynamic primary colors and circular walls at varying heights.
Photograph by Steve Hopson

Fayez S. Sarofim Research Building

BNIM Architects

Completed in 2007, the Fayez S. Sarofim Research Building represents a breakthrough in modern research facilities. Conceived as a new model of science and research predicated on collaboration, place and sustainability, the Fayez S. Sarofim Research Building addresses form and function holistically, encouraging interdisciplinary teamwork in a cooperative and largely communal environment.

Influenced by the Jeffersonian ideal of an "academical village," the SRB was designed as a vertical campus and is both a community unto itself and the anchor of a future campus to the west. The lower stratum of the SRB follows BNIM's affinity for large, flexible, open spaces and serves the larger Texas Medical Center community, while the upper tier is secure and accommodates the more specialized activities of distinct research communities.

FACING PAGE: The northeast façade and street-level entrance to the Fayez S. Sarofim Research Building present a progressive aesthetic, which is reflective of the facility's superior research capabilities.
Project Design Team: Steve McDowell, Mark Shapiro and Casey Cassias.
Photograph by Farshid Assassi

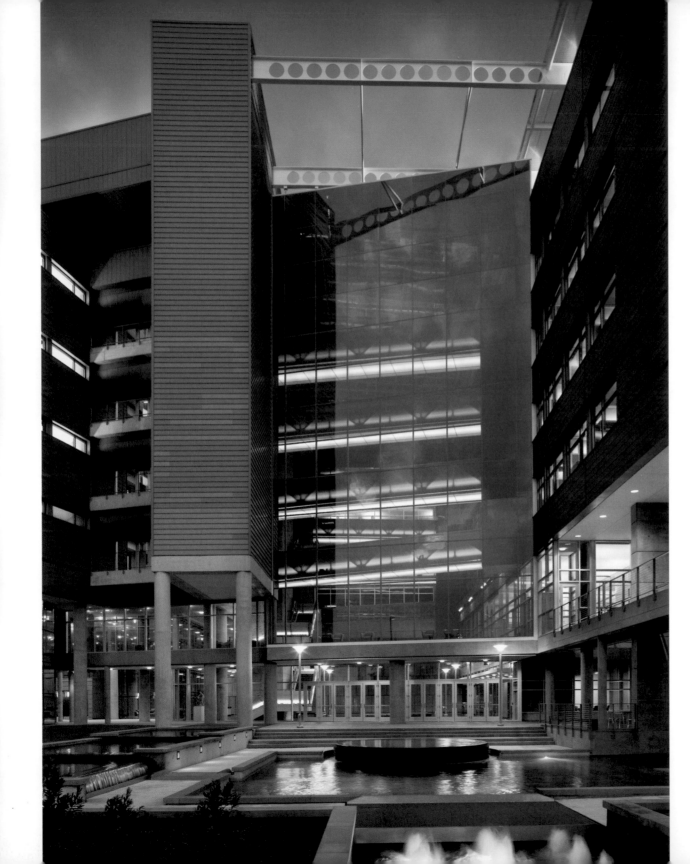

The ground-level central atrium, known as the Hall of Discovery, is positioned between administrative and laboratory wings. Designed as a gateway to the campus, it serves as the common link between interior and exterior spaces and upper and lower strata. Enclosed largely in glass, the atrium and other ground-level spaces form the heart of the future campus, housing a 200-seat auditorium and conference facilities with views and pathways to the outdoor terrace and water feature.

By separating the research and administrative wings, floor-to-floor heights were optimized for both office and laboratory spaces, thus reducing the building volume and further enabling the environmental control system to capture and reuse energy that would normally be wasted. The research wing hosts flexible wet and dry laboratories, as well as specialized shared equipment, and was carefully engineered to isolate vibration that would impact research at the molecular level. Stairs, ramps and bridges facilitate circulation and encourage casual interaction among occupants.

Sustainability is at the heart of every BNIM-designed project, and the Fayez S. Sarofim Research Building is no exception. The structure was oriented within a tight urban site for optimal solar orientation and natural light penetration. The building's fenestration and shading characteristics are configured for each façade's individual position. Innovative air circulation saves energy costs; the research wing requires exceptionally high air quality and is conditioned. This air is filtered and recirculated into the administrative wing and then cycled through the atrium, which is tempered rather than conditioned. The glass in the atrium, as well as throughout the building, is fritted low-E glass, utilized to reduce solar heat gain. The reinforced concrete structure consists of a high fly-ash content mix, and natural, durable materials were used for cladding and finishes.

An exemplary model of sustainability, the careful planning and intelligently considered design by BNIM Architects gave The University of Texas Health Science Center at Houston a first-rate institution that will contribute to disease prevention and healthier lives for future generations—and is restorative for both people and the planet. ■ ■ ■ ■ ■ ■ ■ ■ ■ ■

ABOVE: The auditorium and lecture hall of the SRB feature performance-quality acoustics and ceiling-height windows with views to the landscape.
Photograph by Farshid Assassi

RIGHT: Stairs and bridges in the open central atrium form pathways between the laboratory and office wings.
Photograph by Farshid Assassi

FACING PAGE: The central atrium opens to an exterior courtyard and water feature.
Photograph by Farshid Assassi

Kelly Lane Middle School

■ ■

SHW Group - Austin

■ ■ ■ ■ ■ ■ ■ ■ ■ ■ For years Pflugerville was known primarily as Austin's rural neighbor to the north. However, over the past 20 years Pflugerville has undergone a pronounced transition from farming community to technologically advanced city, buoyed by the nearby presence of Dell's corporate headquarters. SHW Group, a firm dedicated to creating forward-thinking, multifunctional learning environments, has been Pflugerville ISD's sole architect for the past 20 years, having grown with the city throughout the transition and designed a number of its educational facilities. Seeking a new middle school that would be cost-effective, reflective of the city's continued growth and able to support community functions in a sustainable structure, the mutually favorable collaboration between PISD and SHW Group continued, culminating in an ideal architectural solution for the school district's and community's needs.

ABOVE: As a composition within the landscape, Kelly Lane Middle School gives a face to academia.
Photograph by Mark Trew

FACING PAGE: This colorful play on light and materiality helps present a sense of drama, creating a memorable sequence of entry.
Project Design Team: Christian Owens, Vandana Nayak, Cristy Bickel and Scott Reed.
Photograph by Mark Trew

After developing a detailed design program of spaces, primarily the number of classrooms required, SHW Group facilitated a five-day forum between architect, students, teachers, administrators and community members, allowing the local community and school patrons to take ownership in creating its design. The community voice called for multifunctional spaces available for community use as well as flexible, open learning environments in a sustainable structure aesthetically apropos of the city's burgeoning high-tech identity.

The desired progressive appearance was achieved through use of profuse glass, including a striking, glazed front façade, which is capped by a sloped, composite metal roof projection. The transparent nature of the front entry also presents a welcoming aura to patrons and grandly exhibits the heart of the school, the library-media center. The building's unique form and machine-like material elements were delicately balanced with ample stone and masonry, which are durable materials evocative of Pflugerville's rustic heritage.

Interior spaces were designed to be highly adaptable, so that in the event the school requires a dozen more classrooms or six more science labs at some point in the future, the transition can occur seamlessly. This flexibility was achieved by incorporating a rather simple structural grid and designing classrooms sans load-bearing walls—classrooms are built with just stud and gypsum board walls—allowing one classroom to become two, or vice versa, within moments.

Communal meeting areas exist in the media center, gymnasium and cafetorium all of which are located near the front entry so that they have separate access, providing community members entry via an individual, secure entrance outside of normal school hours. The cafetorium's walls are glass, bathing the interior with light while providing views and a connection to an adjacent park. Natural light further imbues interiors via clerestory windows in the inner commons, student corridors and gym. The student corridors, each of which houses a single grade level, feature breakout spaces that allow students to interact with each other outside of the formal classroom setting.

SHW Group's design for Kelly Lane Middle School incorporated the local community in the design process from the onset and provided Pflugerville ISD with a multifunctional, sustainable learning environment that aesthetically captures the city's ongoing transition from rural to suburban and high-tech in an innovative, enduring form. ■ ■ ■ ■ ■ ■ ■ ■ ■ ■ ■

RIGHT: Visitors are welcomed into an expanded hallway, promoting interaction and exchange among students, parents and staff. Flooded with natural light, this space redefines the notion of hallway.
Photograph by Mark Trew

FACING PAGE LEFT: A delicate juxtaposition of steel and glass creates a large south-facing canopy, portraying lightness, transparency and access from within the dining area.
Photograph by Mark Trew

FACING PAGE RIGHT: Interior spaces are defined by the balance between strong, prominent materials—brick, deep bulkheads, rich colors—and the lightness of floor-to-ceiling glass walls.
Photograph by Mark Trew

Saltillo Lofts

■ ■

The Hailey Group

■ ■ ■ ■ ■ ■ ■ ■ ■ ■ The successful completion of the Saltillo Lofts in east Austin represented the first transit-oriented development in the city and served as a catalyst to revitalizing this formerly industrial area. A part of Austin's S.M.A.R.T. Housing™ program—Safe, Mixed-income, Accessible, Reasonably priced, Transit-oriented—the Saltillo Lofts project also adhered to Austin's Green Building Program and is rooted in tenants championed by Envision Central Texas, a nonprofit organization dedicated to sensible growth in the region. The Hailey Group's design for Saltillo Lofts has provided a model for economical, sustainable and desirable multifamily urban housing.

FACING PAGE: The first transit-oriented development in Austin to be constructed adjacent to a future commuter rail station, the Saltillo Lofts provides convenient access to the forthcoming Capitol MetroRail.
Project Design Team: Trey Hailey, Kit Johnson and Susan Daniels.
Photograph by Tre Dunham

Set on a brownfield site that had been home to an abandoned gas station, the Saltillo Lofts project procured an environmental cleanup of the area and represents a valuable reuse of land. As the first project in the Saltillo district, an urban village being planned for east Austin, the development features a mix of commercial space, affordable housing and two-story lofts located directly across from a forthcoming light-rail commuter station and the Lance Armstrong Bikeway.

Beyond reusing a post-industrial site oriented toward transit services, the development sought to achieve an aesthetically interesting, vibrant appeal on apartment-grade construction prices. This led to the design of spartanly finished, loft-like units with exposed building systems. Concrete floors on the first and second level are durable and low-maintenance, as are the structural wood floors on the third floor. Exposed wood trusses, water pipes and requisite systems add interest and become a part of the design. Aluminum-clad wood windows, steel balconies and steel and wood shading devices give the building added architectural character.

Other sustainable project elements include: the use of low VOC-emitting materials; an air-conditioning system prudently selected and customized to be efficient; a light-colored roof to mitigate solar heat gain; insulated wood windows with lots of shading; water-conserving landscaping; and the use of fluorescent lighting.

First-floor retail at the Saltillo Lofts helps create an active streetscape in addition to providing affordable real estate in close proximity to downtown for creative minds to use for gallery space, shops, exhibits, office space, etc. Above the commercial space there is a mix of two-story lofts and affordable units. The affordable units make up 40 percent of the residences and all enjoy views to the development's courtyard.

The winner of a stewardship award from Envision Central Texas, Saltillo Lofts has revitalized a significant area of east Austin, providing affordable, sustainable and urbane housing moments from Austin's vibrant downtown. ■ ■ ■ ■ ■ ■ ■ ■ ■ ■

RIGHT: Saltillo Lofts is a key component in revitalizing what had been a rather lifeless part of east Austin.
Photograph by Hailey Mar

FACING PAGE LEFT: The development includes eclectic ground-level retail offerings under a variety of loft-style units.
Photograph by Hailey Mar

FACING PAGE RIGHT: Aluminum-clad windows along with steel balconies and shading devices provide exterior character.
Photograph by Tre Dunham

Walnut Bend Elementary School

■ ■

VLK Architects

■ ■ ■ ■ ■ ■ ■ ■ ■ ■ After nearly a half-century's existence, a longstanding Houston school in a well-established neighborhood received a pertinent, overdue replacement—integrally planned around a host of sustainable technologies—preserving mature trees while greatly enhancing school facilities and the local community.

In 2002 Houston voters approved a multimillion-dollar bond issue to rebuild and upgrade many facilities within the Houston Independent School District, including Walnut Bend Elementary School, which was rebuilt on its existing site as designed by VLK Architects. As part of the bond package, Walnut Bend was selected as one of two schools to serve as a case study for building LEED-certified schools in HISD.

FACING PAGE: Walnut Bend Elementary School was one of the first schools in the Houston area to strive for LEED certification.
Photograph by Geoffrey Lyon

Built in 1960, the original school was characterized by exposed conduits, old systems and a strong need for more space; the number of students in its attendance zone had outgrown the facility's capacity to the point that more classes were being held in portable buildings than the original structure. There was also no on-site parking or designated drop-off zones for students, which was one of many concerns for the site-based committee of teachers, principals, parents and community members that participated in a series of meetings with VLK.

Set on a modest five-acre site, a two-story design was selected to fully facilitate HISD's 84,500-square-foot program for elementary schools. The configuration also supported a one-way drive—with separate drop-off and pick-up areas for students—with parking that loops in and through the site, moving traffic off neighborhood streets. The two-story configuration also provided areas for three distinctive age-appropriate playgrounds and preserved a host of mature trees on site including oaks, sycamores and pines.

With LEED certification in mind, material remnants from the demolition of the original Walnut Bend were salvaged and construction waste was recycled; local and regional materials from nearby sources were employed as much as possible. Native landscaping mixes were used outside; terrazzo floors throughout the interior are durable and low maintenance, and low VOC- and odor-emitting paints, adhesives and floor coverings comprise much of the interior. The building's mechanical systems utilize computerized control systems to shut off when not in use and light switches use occupancy sensors to avoid wasting energy; energy recovery wheels recapture energy as it is exhausted from the building for reuse.

VLK Architects' design and planning resulted in a superior Walnut Bend Elementary School with greater capacity, improved circulation and sustainable technologies. The new school gave teachers and students a more efficient, user-friendly learning environment benefitting the local community. ■ ■ ■ ■ ■ ■ ■ ■ ■ ■

RIGHT: The outdoor nature center extends non-traditional learning opportunities to students via ponds and other hands-on educational tools.
Photograph by Geoffrey Lyon

FACING PAGE LEFT: The school's main entrance is a blend of aluminum and glass, which is contrasted by two tones of brick veneer.
Photograph by Chad M. Davis, AIA

FACING PAGE RIGHT: The lobby features a tree and a terrazzo floor design with poems and facts about the school mascot, the bald eagle.
Photograph by Chad M. Davis, AIA

Warren Skaaren Environmental Learning Center at Westcave Preserve

■ ■

Jackson & McElhaney Architects

■ ■ ■ ■ ■ ■ ■ ■ ■ ■ An extraordinary, multipurpose educational facility that models conservation and utilizes durable, low-maintenance forms, the Warren Skaaren Environmental Learning Center at Westcave Preserve is an award-winning structure planned and designed by Jackson & McElhaney Architects. Its simplicity in form and materials blends in ideally with the remarkable terrain of the preserve and exhibits valuable sustainable design concepts in an economically viable structure.

Efforts began in the late 1990s to create a world-class educational facility promoting stewardship, reflective of an incredible nature preserve 30 miles west of Austin. A 30-acre tract featuring two distinctive ecosystems, the preserve features semiarid uplands found throughout central Texas along lush riparian

FACING PAGE: The center's simple forms comprised of natural materials blend impeccably with the terrain of the Westcave Preserve.
Project Design Team: Robert Jackson and Michael McElhaney.
Photograph by Casey Dunn Photography

canyons and amazing natural features such as a 40-foot waterfall and 600-year-old cypress trees. The preserve is home to myriad plant and animal species, such as the endangered golden-cheeked warbler.

At 3,000 square feet the learning center is a simple yet durable, open-ended structure that opens to a 1,750-square-foot terrace overlooking a canyon. The building was largely inspired by the gracious, enduring structures built by the Civilian Conservation Corps during the 1930s, which were efficient, comprised of natural materials and integrally connected with the landscape. The structure employs locally quarried Glenrose stone, which is filled with fossils, and the walls are used for "fossil hunts" in which kids literally climb the walls searching for ammonites and other remnants of past epochs. Additional building components include naturally finished stucco panels, interior pine decking derived from Texas forests, lasting, low-maintenance terrazzo floors and standing-seam roofs for durability and rainwater collection.

Used day and night, seven days a week, the learning center is capable of accommodating 150-plus students while hosting smaller visitor groups and serving as a community center. Viewed as three-dimensional textbooks, valuable educational exhibits afford opportunities for learning about an array of pertinent topics such as wildlife study and observation, endangered species, biology, geology, astronomy, water harvesting, history and more. From a trip to

TOP LEFT: The classroom area utilizes a folding glass wall, which allows for multiple functions without losing visual contact with the site.
Photograph by Casey Dunn Photography

BOTTOM LEFT: The clerestory band along the entry walk allows indirect natural light to filter into the space. The roof appears to float above stone cisterns and ancillary spaces.
Photograph by Greg Hursley

FACING PAGE: The terraced stone seating outside the south entry provides an engaging space that is used as one of the outdoor classrooms.
Photograph by Casey Dunn Photography

Rome and seeing the Santa Maria degli Angeli Church's famous meridian line, Robert Jackson, AIA, brought back the idea for a similar concept in the learning center's unique solar exhibit. A one-inch hole in the exhibit's ceiling produces a small spot of sunlight on the floor during midday, which can then be tracked via a meridian line traversing the visitor's center, exhibiting the earth's movement and illustrating numerous fundamental principles.

Sustainability was of course at the heart of the project and is evidenced in all aspects. A five-cistern rainwater collection and filtration system demonstrates water quality and cycles; wetlands and composting toilets demonstrate recycling of materials in nature; and energy conservation is manifested through photovoltaics, daylighting, ground-source heat pumps, quality insulation and overhangs—a sampling of the many sustainable elements. A recipient of seven design awards, including an AIA Committee on the Environment Top Ten Green Project for 2006, the facility has provided a true community center wholly dedicated to environmental education. ■ ■ ■ ■ ■ ■ ■ ■ ■ ■ ■

West Brazos Junior High School

SHW Group - Houston

■ ■ ■ ■ ■ ■ ■ ■ ■ ■ West Brazos Junior High School is a consummate example of how an exciting learning environment can be achieved in an ecologically mindful building built on tight budget parameters. Working with Columbia-Brazoria ISD, SHW Group designed this new academic facility to be flexible, durable and sustainable, and when completed in May 2006 West Brazos Junior High School became the first public school in Texas to receive LEED certification.

Set on an undeveloped, 53-acre parcel with 90-plus native trees in Brazoria, Texas, the school was carefully sited to reduce the number of trees that would be removed and nearly all affected trees were replaced. The trees were used to strategically shade the parking lot and the sidewalk to minimize heat gain from the paving, as well as provide shade in the courtyard near the cafeteria. Native wetlands on site were preserved and provide a valuable

FACING PAGE: West Brazos Junior High School in Columbia-Brazoria ISD is the first public school in Texas to receive LEED certification.
Project Design Team: Jennifer Henrikson, Ruben Araujo, Luis Fernandez and Frank Kelly.
Photograph by Richard Payne, FAIA

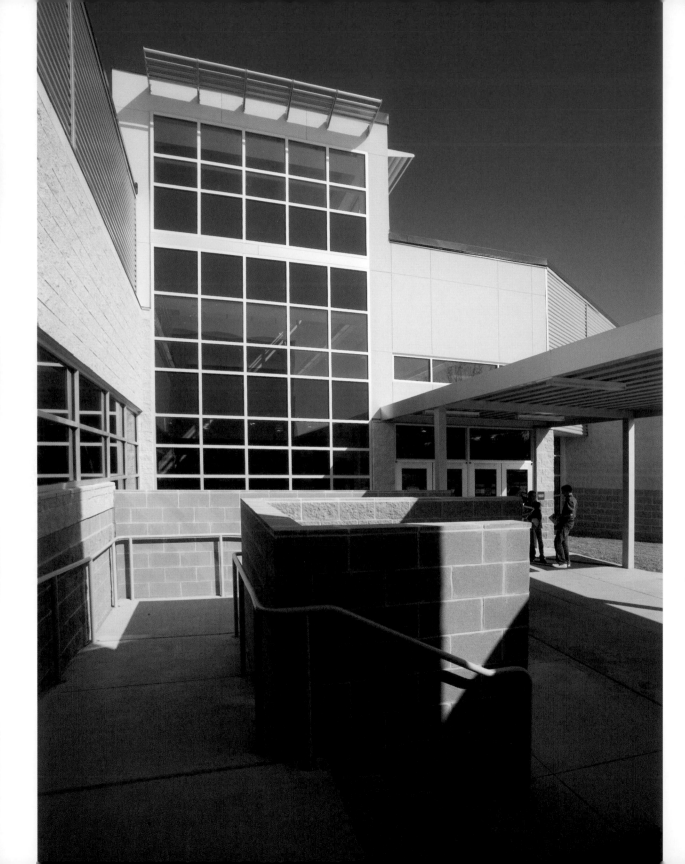

outdoor learning environment for the science wing, which is oriented adjacent to the wetlands. A large detention pond was placed to collect rainwater, which is then distributed back into the control utility infrastructure while hearty, native vegetation diminishes irrigation needs.

The exterior is comprised largely of concrete masonry, chosen for its natural, durable quality, and is accented by stucco and metal panels, which are economical, resilient and low-maintenance. An Energy Star roof provides high reflectance and low emissivity, limiting the amount of heat penetrating the building. A thermally efficient wall design is aided by windows with low-E glazing to mitigate heat gain, and horizontal shading devices reduce direct glare but also distribute natural light further into learning spaces. Natural colors of beiges, browns and rusts complemented by these low-maintenance materials allow the building to blend with the beauty of the heavily wooded campus.

Inside, West Brazos is organized along a long circulation spine that connects multiple academic/activity pod centers. This main corridor includes clerestory lighting and wood decking, bringing a sense of warmth to the space. Ceramic tile on the corridor walls is durable and easy to clean yet not institutional-feeling like concrete or cinder block walls. Low VOC-emitting floor materials with a high recycled content are also durable and require minimal maintenance.

LEFT: Locally manufactured materials comprise more than 55 percent of the school's building materials, which positively impacted the local economy and reduced long-distance transportation emissions.
Photograph by Richard Payne, FAIA

FACING PAGE TOP: The circulation spine features clerestory windows, allowing natural light to penetrate deep into the core spaces, which reduces artificial lighting requirements and energy costs.
Photograph by Richard Payne, FAIA

FACING PAGE BOTTOM: With gracious views of the wooded landscape, open arrangement of the furniture and plenty of natural light, the library provides students with a motivating learning environment.
Photograph by Richard Payne, FAIA

Throughout the entire school spaces were architecturally designed to be exceptionally flexible, which maximizes the potential uses of many different areas. For example, the cafeteria and fine arts wing are separated by a stage with a movable partition, so instead of the additional expense to provide an auditorium, the cafeteria seating area is used for fine arts performances and general assembly-type of functions. Dedicated flex space in the classroom pods, light-filled from clerestories above, provides an ideal setting for breakout teaching or group instruction.

An exciting learning environment based on sustainable technologies within limited monetary means, SHW Group's design for West Brazos Junior High School illustrates how to successfully create an engaging, economical and eco-friendly school. ■ ■ ■ ■ ■ ■ ■ ■ ■ ■ ■

World Birding Center

Lake | Flato Architects

■ ■ ■ ■ ■ ■ ■ ■ ■ Set upon 60 acres of rich and fertile terrain in the Lower Rio Grande Valley, the World Birding Center headquarters at Mission represents the simple yet effective use of local materials and landscape to preserve habitat and provide a restorative and welcoming environment for myriad species of birds and butterflies. Designed by Lake I Flato Architects, the World Birding Center is a grand symbol of sustainable design—it was named a 2006 AIA Committee on the Environment Top 10 Green Project—and has helped minimize impact, restore habitat and highlight native habitat preservation.

ABOVE: The old irrigation canal, which forms the boundary between the visitor center and the preserved habitat, serves as a reminder of the region's dependence on water from the Rio Grande River.
Photograph by Hester + Hardaway

FACING PAGE: The visitor center offers many spaces from which to observe wildlife activity, from the glass-enclosed café to the shaded walkways that connect the buildings.
Project Design Team: David Lake, Robert Harris, Roy Schweers, Darryl Ohlenbusch, Isabel Mijangos, Heather DeGrella and Margaret Sledge.
Photograph by Hester + Hardaway

The Rio Grande Valley, actually a river delta despite its valley appellation, has in the past century lost 95 percent of its native habitat, experienced dramatic water problems and issues related to the Rio Grande's flow, endured increased air and water pollution and witnessed the forced migration and even eradication of species. Recognizing this ongoing crisis, Lake I Flato strove to minimize the effects associated with constructing the WBC headquarters and visitor center on this precious site and to restore landscape, thereby inviting various avian species, butterflies, dragonflies and other wildlife to be in close contact with visitors.

The design approach was a complex of buildings loosely connected via a network of arbors and trellises, reflective of an agricultural vernacular indigenous to the region. Lake I Flato sited the WBC on the corner of the parcel next to a canal, creating a modest oasis to support the expansive preserve. The buildings were viewed as the backdrop and support mechanism to the natural habitat, which is the draw—the habitat itself, not the structures.

Building costs were minimized to provide funds for landscape improvements, benefiting both humans and migrating species. The original 20,000-square-foot program was reduced to 13,000 square feet, providing a 35-percent reduction in building materials, energy and maintenance, and the use of barrel vaults required 48 percent less steel than a conventional steel structure. The network of connecting arbors and trellises further reduced need for materials and air-conditioned spaces. The buildings were sited parallel to the canal to catch prevailing summer breezes while deep porches block the sun, and buildings were clustered to create shady green spaces and enhance the indoor-outdoor relationship. Local, natural materials like clay block and brick from Mexico were employed for durability and cost effectiveness. A 47,000-gallon rainwater collection system is used for irrigation while rainwater guzzlers, natural pools and

water seeps provide water for birds and butterflies. The flooded habitat demonstration garden is a focal point; it mimics the natural currents of flooding that once occurred on the Rio Grande River, creating an ideal habitat for many varied species.

The World Birding Center has effectively restored precious natural habitat and seen a growth in the types and number of bird species and butterflies, providing a premier destination for eco-enthusiasts to enjoy this amazing natural habitat. ■ ■ ■ ■ ■ ■ ■ ■ ■ ■ ■

ABOVE LEFT: Metal cisterns store up to 47,000 gallons of rainwater, which are then used to irrigate the landscape.
Photograph by Hester + Hardaway

ABOVE RIGHT: The café offers respite from the heat and sun while still providing connections to the outdoors.
Photograph by Hester + Hardaway

FACING PAGE: Corrugated, arched metal roof panels, inspired by agricultural buildings, double as roof material and structure. Local clay block and brick are used to create walls.
Photograph by Hester + Hardaway

CHAPTER SIX
City Futures

If a modern-day city sprung up through the creative genius of one architect alone—regardless of how talented he or she may be—it would pale in comparison to one that evolved over decades, even centuries, and was touched by the hands of many. The most spectacular cities in the world boast an eclectic mixture of architectural styles, from classical to contemporary, and it is the architect's prerogative to reinvent these broad genres to tailor a building's aesthetic appearance and functionality to the current and future needs of those who will interact with it on a daily basis.

A great deal of trust and communication is required for a group of people to conceptualize and develop plans for works of architecture that may not be tangibly built until many years down the road. HKS' new Dallas Cowboys Stadium, Ziegler Cooper Architects' The Austonian and Beeler Guest Owens Architects' The Mercantile are a few illustrious examples. The collective realized visions of past architects provide an exquisite tapestry into which the masterpieces we call contemporary art may be harmoniously woven.

Enjoy these products of research, inspiration and diligence that will culminate in remarkable buildings integrally intertwined into our urban fabric. Take a glimpse of what is yet to come through these dynamic drawings, blueprints and renderings.

Legal Aid of NorthWest Texas, MULTATECH, page 308

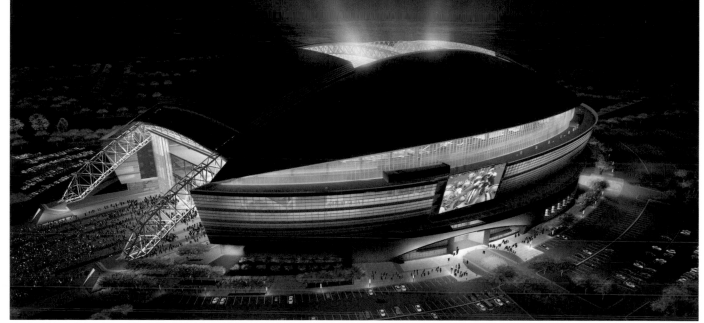

Dallas Cowboys Stadium, HKS, Inc., page 284

Art Village on Main

The Warren Group Architects, Inc.

■ ■ ■ ■ ■ ■ ■ ■ ■ ■ As a local community, McAllen has in recent years placed a strong emphasis on art to go along with its longstanding traditions of community and family interaction. The first Friday of every month brings an eclectic exhibition of local art, in a variety of mediums, as talented individuals throughout the Rio Grande Valley and beyond present their work at businesses in the heart of the city's art district. Aiming to further develop this pertinent area of town, local developers Alonzo Cantu and Yolanda Cantu, in collaboration with The Warren Group Architects, are revitalizing a full city block to greatly enhance this center of culture and creativity, providing the community with a sense of place and a flourishing arts district.

ABOVE: Building B on Main Street invites visitors to the open plaza through a wide, covered walkway, allowing a view of the landscape and other buildings.
Rendering by Laura Nassri Warren

FACING PAGE: A succession of arched entryways and heavily landscaped sidewalks and breezeways reflect the area's Mediterranean and Hispanic flair.
Project Design Team: Laura Nassri Warren, Andrina Garza, Claudio A. Leon and Amanda D. Gomez.
Rendering by Laura Nassri Warren

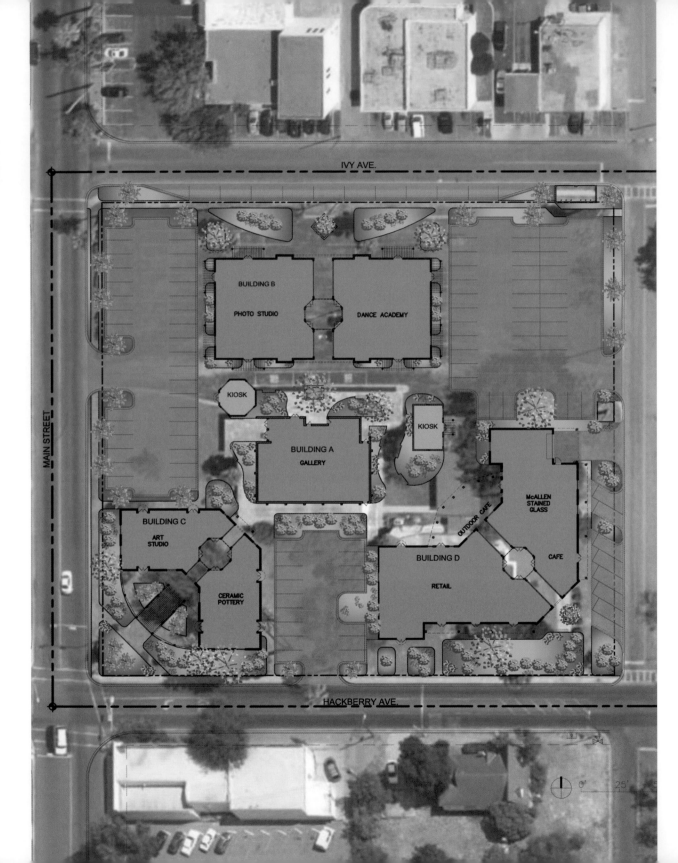

IVY AVE.

MAIN STREET

BUILDING B

PHOTO STUDIO

DANCE ACADEMY

KIOSK

KIOSK

BUILDING A

GALLERY

BUILDING C

ART STUDIO

CERAMIC POTTERY

OUTDOOR CAFE

McALLEN STAINED GLASS

BUILDING D

RETAIL

CAFE

HACKBERRY AVE.

0'   25'

A self-guided tour of art galleries and art hosts in one of the city's oldest areas, the McAllen ArtWalk has provided excellent opportunities since 2004 to meet new people sharing a passion for art while highlighting the rich culture of the community. Currently a sea of asphalt after the demolition of some dilapidated buildings, the block includes an old funeral home in the center, which will be retrofitted, and upon completion will include four additional buildings, several kiosks and abundant outdoor space adorned with lush, native landscaping. The monthly ArtWalk features graphic art, sculpture, theater, music, dance and other genres, which are hosted at local businesses and galleries. The redeveloped block will feature separate buildings devoted to a photography studio, dance studio, painting studio, jewelry outfit and a depot of glass and stained glass. Each of these structures will not only sell and/or exhibit art but also provide educational opportunities to teach patrons in these various mediums.

The structures will pay homage to the culture via local architecture, which will be reflective of the region along with some Hispanic and Mediterranean nuances. Comprised of clay tile, stucco and stone, the structures will be wholly reflective of the local flavor. Many of the old doors and windows were reclaimed from the original buildings—along with copious asphalt from the street—and will be applied to the new structures, adding great character. Public green space will be an integral component of the development, comprising approximately 30 percent of the area, and will provide great outdoor gathering areas, particularly for the enjoyment of concerts and performances. Of course, public art will be prevalent around every corner, with the centerpiece being a vibrant mural placed in an existent building's entrance that will feature stained glass and glass beads encrusted in a plaster mural, which will tell a part of the history of McAllen.

Highlighting local art for the people, by the people, The Warren Group Architects' efforts are helping to expose local artistry and promote education in the arts by providing an area that will attract tourism and be of enduring value to the people of the Rio Grande Valley. ■ ■ ■ ■ ■ ■ ■ ■ ■ ■

TOP: An old funeral home is converted into an art gallery and renovated to fit into the context; the building will display a mural designed by Yolanda Cantu.
Rendering by Laura Nassri Warren

BOTTOM: The arcaded patios of Building D maintain a romantic feeling with pure Hispanic forms, creating transparent, open spaces with extensive views.
Rendering by Laura Nassri Warren

FACING PAGE: The overall site plan depicts an interpretation of traditional Hispanic courtyards and patios running through the multiple buildings set around a plaza and renovated building.
Graphic by Amanda Gomez

The Austonian

Ziegler Cooper Architects

■ ■ ■ ■ ■ ■ ■ ■ ■ ■ At 58 stories and 683 feet tall upon completion in 2009, The Austonian, a high-rise residential and retail project, will tower above neighboring structures and be the defining element of the Austin skyline. In a city that has long eschewed extensive urban development—particularly that of a high-rise nature—it was an initiative brought forth by Mayor Will Wynn and the Austin City Council encouraging density and urban living in downtown that initially set the stage for such a grand endeavor. But beyond this paradigm shift, it took an extensive commitment to designing and building green to secure the litany of approvals needed to erect such a monumental structure in downtown Austin.

The Austonian was originally conceived in response to Mayor Wynn's vision of adding 25,000 new urban residents to downtown Austin over a 10-year period, which would result in considerable local economic and ecological benefits, among many such considerations. A design competition for the

FACING PAGE: One of the building's many amenities is the aqua level, located at the top of a 90-foot podium, which affords a dramatic view of the Capitol.
Project Design Team: Kurt T. Hull, R. Scott Ziegler, Chris Petrash, Rafael Feinstein, Fani Qano, Sameer Balvally, Manuel Navarro, John Paul Garland and Charles Middlebrooks.
Rendering by Diamond Computer Graphics Co., Ltd.

ambitious mixed-use project concluded with the selection of Ziegler Cooper Architects and the firm's design of a captivating, elliptical-shaped tower. The setting, a 29,000-square-foot site at the corner of Congress Avenue and Second Street, challenged the architect with housing 187 luxury condominiums, parking, retail and luxury amenities on one-third of a city block while adhering to Capitol View Corridor restrictions, which protect views from all vantages to the Texas State Capitol.

An essential and early zoning provision enabled a more generous floor-to-area ratio on the project site—approximately three times the previously permitted ratio—which allowed a structure with a 10,000-square-foot building footprint to attain such extraordinary height. Of course, designing such a tall and skinny structure presented exceptional engineering challenges, which were overcome via a series of wind analyses that led to the incorporation of cross bracing on two floors, astutely sized columns and structural systems, and a dampening device atop the structure to minimize swaying.

The design calls for a lively retail scene on the first two floors, which are set under six floors devoted to parking. From there the tower portion of The Austonian begins, dedicated primarily to luxury condominiums. The tower's 10th floor is an

LEFT: The building, near Town Lake in the heart of the city, consists of a retail and parking podium and a tall, slender elliptical residential tower with illuminated crown.
Rendering by Diamond Computer Graphics Co., Ltd.

FACING PAGE LEFT: As The Austonian rises, the layers of façade peel back to reveal the crown—adorned with an observation deck, private party rooms and fitness center—with unparalleled views of the city, lake and Hill Country.
Rendering by Diamond Computer Graphics Co., Ltd.

FACING PAGE RIGHT: Among the many green features are rainwater-retention system and native planting, high-performance glass, permanent shading devices and green roofs.
Rendering by Diamond Computer Graphics Co., Ltd.

amenity level offering attractions such as a wine room, lounge and a small cinema area. Also on the 10th floor is an exquisitely landscaped outdoor urban garden with a green roof, 75-foot pool, herb gardens, sundeck, barbecue grill, dog park—all with views of the State Capitol—providing an ideal setting for outdoor leisure. Another green roof is located on the 55th floor sky lounge and outdoor terrace, and sustainability was an integral component of the design, which is part of the Austin Green Building Program. The 56th level is a fitness center with 360-degree views of the Hill Country. The entire building

is adorned with high-performance, low-E glass and utilizes MechoShades, Energy Star-rated appliances and a rainwater capture system, among many green elements.

Soon to be the iconic structure in the downtown skyline, The Austonian represents a bold move toward a denser downtown environment, overcoming significant challenges in a green design that is uniquely Austin. ■ ■ ■ ■ ■ ■ ■ ■ ■ ■

Corpus Christi Bayfront Master Plan

Gignac Associates

■ ■ ■ ■ ■ ■ ■ ■ ■ ■ In a city with a rich historical fabric spanning more than a century and a half, the sparkling blue waters of Corpus Christi Bay have long served as the backdrop to the city's hustle and bustle. Nearly a decade into the 21st century, Corpus Christi is getting an overhaul that will ensure the bay remains an integral part of the city's vitality, improving opportunities to enjoy it daily.

Endeavoring to revitalize the heart of Corpus Christi, a 2.5-mile-long waterfront expanse along Shoreline Drive fronting Corpus Christi Bay, the city commissioned Gignac Associates, in collaboration with Sasaki, TVS and Arquitectonica, to master plan this pertinent stretch with an emphasis on the pedestrian experience.

ABOVE: The redevelopment centers on a 2.5-mile-long waterfront expanse along Shoreline Drive fronting majestic Corpus Christi Bay.
Rendering by Sasaki

FACING PAGE: Vibrant pedestrian zones, such as a waterfront café under a unique shade structure, will be prominently featured in the revitalized downtown and marina area.
Project Design Team: Raymond Gignac and Paul Rybalka, Gignac Associates; Alan Ward and Jason S. Hellendrung, Sasaki; Robert Gignac, Gignac Landscape Architects; Kevin Gordon, TVS.
Rendering by TVS

Community involvement was deemed essential with this substantial undertaking, and a dialog with local citizens took root via more than 30 meetings in which imperative community input was gleaned. Many had reservations about transforming what had long been a fairly traditional ocean drive, but considering the public's concerns and desires helped procure a plan with safe, usable green space by the water while accommodating patrons to the downtown/marina area with a mix of passive and active spaces.

The design team created a master plan that starts at McGee Beach on the south side of downtown, first moving Shoreline Drive to the west, providing additional park space adjacent to the beach. Moving northward, all lanes of Ocean Drive will be set right next to the water, which accomplishes two goals. Ocean Drive's original configuration was characterized by multiple lanes of 55-plus mile-per-hour traffic flanking an

80-foot-wide median, centering a generous expanse of green space between dangerous thoroughfares, making it largely unusable. Many citizens emphasized that they enjoy Ocean Drive vistas from their car while driving and did not want to lose that aspect of in-town commuting. Relocating Ocean Drive such that it abuts the water enhances the experience for drivers and grasps that valuable green space from the clutches of danger, making it usable.

Moving Shoreline Drive close to the water in front of the downtown/marina area enabled the creation of one-block park spaces, providing intimate pockets capable of hosting small venues or leisurely recreation. Scale was a great consideration in devising this assembly of smaller green spaces, as it will allow for a much more intimate setting in the vibrant downtown and marina area. These engaging pedestrian zones will feature

interactive water features, arbors, gardens, a small-scale café and unique architecture such as the nearby convention center, which was also designed by Gignac Associates in association with TVS and Arquitectonica.

The master plan will also create an arrival feature where the well-traveled Interstate 37 meets the water, creating a sense of destination upon entrance into Corpus Christi.

Greatly enhancing the downtown Corpus Christi experience, the bayfront master plan carefully crafted by the design team featuring Gignac Associates will be of long-term benefit to the city and local community, ensuring Corpus Christi Bay remains integrally intertwined with the city's liveliness for generations to come. ■ ■ ■ ■ ■ ■ ■ ■ ■ ■

ABOVE: Carefully planned, one-block park spaces will afford an array of opportunities for passive recreation, including small-scale cafés on the waterfront, maintaining the destination's vitality for future generations. Rendering by TVS

FACING PAGE: Conceived as an inland beach, this interactive water feature is just one of many planned components of an enhanced, pedestrian-oriented bayfront, the heart of Corpus Christi. Rendering by Sasaki

Dallas Cowboys Stadium

■■■■■■■■■■■■■■■■■■■■■■■■■■■■■■■■■■■

HKS, Inc.

■■■■■■■■■■ When Dallas Cowboys owner Jerry Jones decided to build a new stadium for his world-renowned football team, he envisioned a structure that was event-flexible, high-capacity, architecturally innovative and unique, and more than anything, a fitting home for such an iconic, storied franchise. After holding a national design competition, which was followed by presentations of preliminary design concepts and a series of interviews, HKS was selected to tackle the extraordinarily ambitious, 2.3-million-square-foot project that is unmatched in scope by any other similar venue.

One of the first requirements that Jones had for his new facility was to maintain the trademark roof opening that has long characterized Texas Stadium, the team's home since 1971. However, unlike Texas Stadium's roof opening, the new stadium in Arlington will feature a retractable roof, making those early-

FACING PAGE: The largest NFL stadium in the world, the Dallas Cowboys Stadium is designed to enhance the international Cowboys brand with its modern, progressive architecture while incorporating elements of the Texas Stadium-era Cowboys' heritage, such as the trademark roof opening and the Ring of Honor.
Project Design Team: Bryan Trubey, Mark Williams and Craig Stockwell.
Rendering courtesy of HKS, Inc.

season games and other mid-year events held there significantly more bearable during north Texas' heat waves.

A patron to the new Cowboys stadium will immediately notice the pair of quarter-mile-long ground trusses that extend across the length of the stadium. The longest ground span trusses in the world, these two monumental elements are equal in length to the Empire State Building turned on its side. Powerful and unique in their own right, these two trusses also function as the main structural components extending over the playing field, thus enabling them to support the largest high-definition video boards of any NFL stadium.

Cognizant that its main competition was a football fan watching a 50-inch, plasma television screen from 12 feet away, HKS conducted extensive studies to replicate that football-viewing experience. The result was a pair of 180-foot-long by 50-foot-wide video boards that face each sideline. Essentially, patrons to the new Cowboys stadium in Arlington can be confident that the view they are enjoying from their seat is every bit as good—if not demonstrably better—than anything they could replicate at home.

Other innovative features of the new stadium include: six paneled doors in each end zone that are equal in size to a 10-story building, look down upon large, entry plaza areas and open up completely to the outside to accommodate agreeable weather; playing field-level luxury suites that will practically position fans on the sidelines; and an 86-foot-high canted glass wall that sweeps across the venue's elegant exterior skin.

With a normal capacity of 80,000 patrons, the new stadium is also exceptionally flexible, allowing for capacities well over 100,000 for special events, like the Super Bowl, which will be held at the new stadium in 2011. The facility is right on schedule to open for the Cowboys' 2009 regular season, and thanks to Jerry Jones' grand vision combined with the practical genius employed by HKS, the new Cowboys stadium will be a grandiose facility, fitting of America's team and unparalleled by any other stadium anywhere in the world. ■ ■ ■ ■ ■ ■ ■ ■ ■ ■

ABOVE LEFT: The Cowboys' locker room is an all-inclusive destination fitted with custom wood lockers, ceiling-recessed projectors and a video display wall.
Rendering courtesy of HKS, Inc.

ABOVE RIGHT: Two silver-level clubs, at 39,000 square feet each, provide a sophisticated environment with custom detailing.
Rendering courtesy of HKS, Inc.

FACING PAGE TOP: Cowboys fans will be captivated by a one-of-a-kind feature unlike any in the world, a center-hung video board.
Rendering courtesy of HKS, Inc.

FACING PAGE BOTTOM: The end zones feature the largest retractable doors in the world. Each has a five-leaf, translucent retractable opening measuring 120 feet high.
Rendering courtesy of HKS, Inc.

East Avenue

PageSoutherlandPage

In recent years Austin has widely embraced New Urbanism ideals, seeking to add density in the core of the city and eliminate sprawl, growing the city in a sustainable, conscientious manner. When Concordia University decided to relocate its campus, which had occupied a 23-acre site close to downtown and just blocks from the University of Texas, it presented developers with an extraordinary opportunity to establish a high-density, truly mixed-use and sustainable urban community that will be an integral part of central Austin's vitality for decades to come.

Planned and designed by PageSoutherlandPage, the East Avenue development derived its appellation from the name of the street spanning the site, which had for many years been an essential thoroughfare that knitted east side neighborhoods into downtown—before being overshadowed by the presence of the region's foremost traveled highway, nearby Interstate 35. The departure of Concordia University from this valuable parcel affords 2.75

FACING PAGE: An innovative five-star hotel with priorities placed on green building and reflecting local culture is at the hub of the development. Rendering by Pirate Design

million square feet that will eventually include 1,450 residential units, 600,000 square feet of office space, 325,000 square feet of retail space and a 210-room luxury hotel—all of which will be accomplished without harming the rich fabric of nearby tree-lined, single-family neighborhoods featuring many historic homes.

The centerpiece of the community will be a five-star Hyatt Andaz hotel, which will be 180 feet tall and include luxury accommodations, a pool, spa and fitness center as well as a 20,000-square-foot green roof offering residents a veritable "park in the sky." The lush landscaping will be augmented by spectacular views to downtown and the UT campus. The Andaz will be truly eco-friendly and, like all the buildings in the development, will be LEED certified; the hotel is working toward a LEED Gold rating. In addition to the requisite environmentally friendly building materials and systems, the hotel will utilize a sunscreen made from sustainably farmed wood that is akin to setting the building under a large live oak tree, enveloping the building for shading purposes while exuding a warm, inviting tone.

The community will also include a pair of 180-foot-tall multifamily residential towers and a 120-foot-tall office building providing class-A work space, all of which enjoy resplendent views. East Avenue's ground level will feature an enormous amount of retail, entertainment and restaurants, and the community will be highly pedestrian-oriented in general. The placement of streets will correlate with large pecans, oaks and other trees to create a series of miniature urban parks that preserve trees and natural contours to provide verdant outdoor spaces. Along the sidewalks bioswales will include street trees and plant material that cleanse runoff water from the streets and sidewalks, with bridges providing passage over these landscape elements. A single, highly efficient central plant will provide energy for the entire district.

An exciting community that will include a true medley of distinct uses, East Avenue will bring vitality and energy to the core of central Austin while promoting valuable sustainable concepts and in-town density without harming the area's eclectic neighborhood texture. ■ ■ ■ ■ ■ ■ ■ ■ ■

ABOVE: An active retail level is oriented to pedestrians while the contained street space of East Avenue meanders through the development.
Rendering by Pirate Design

RIGHT: An inventive new approach to streetscape development incorporates bioswales and other environmentally progressive features.
Rendering by Pirate Design

FACING PAGE: Multifamily residential towers with long north and south faces optimize solar advantage.
Rendering by Pirate Design

Edinburg City Hall

TAG International

■ ■ ■ ■ ■ ■ ■ ■ ■ Desiring to build a new city hall that would encourage downtown development and strengthen civic identity, Edinburg city officials commissioned TAG International to design the new city hall facility as part of a larger master plan effort. Going beyond the initial project parameters, TAG helped city leaders envision the new structure as part of a larger civic epicenter, creating a sense of identity for Edinburg and an appealing pedestrian destination.

Working with a site featuring several historic buildings including a 1920s-era auditorium that had long served as a community hub, the project team conducted extensive research on the history of the community and its architectural heritage. An early photograph of the old county courthouse was obtained and used as a starting point, and the design grew from the region's historical language, interpreted in a contemporary fashion. The historic

FACING PAGE: An elliptical plaza anchors the existing Edinburg Auditorium, a state historical landmark, with the new facility and will include a three-story tower, which will provide a visible city landmark.
Project Design Team: Bruce Jackson, Ron Pope and Jamie Crawley.
Rendering by M. Brown, courtesy of TAG International

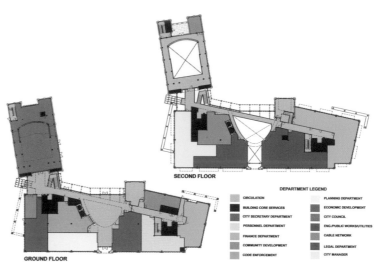

SECOND FLOOR

GROUND FLOOR

DEPARTMENT LEGEND

CIRCULATION	PLANNING DEPARTMENT
BUILDING CORE SERVICES	ECONOMIC DEVELOPMENT
CITY SECRETARY DEPARTMENT	CITY COUNCIL
PERSONNEL DEPARTMENT	ENG./PUBLIC WORKS/UTILITIES
FINANCE DEPARTMENT	CABLE NETWORK
COMMUNITY DEVELOPMENT	LEGAL DEPARTMENT
CODE ENFORCEMENT	CITY MANAGER

auditorium was preserved and made a focus of the overall site design. The auditorium's stone base and brick exterior material palette will be incorporated into the new city hall as a nod to the past.

Planning led to the closing of a portion of McIntyre Street—a thoroughfare that connected the two most prominent structures in the larger community, the county courthouse and the University of Texas-Pan American—for the creation of a pedestrian axis through the two-block site. The new city hall will be sited at the center of that former street such that it relates to the historic auditorium. Because there was no significant outdoor space, the design team incorporated a public plaza, which led to the inclusion of an iconic, three-story tower as part of the city hall, creating a public square evocative of European plazas.

Referencing Baroque architecture, the plaza was designed as an elliptical shape, which is defined by brick pavers and features a porcelain-tile compass star and fountain in the center. The plaza will be brought inside the city hall's two-story main lobby, which is a transparent volume allowing passersby to peer

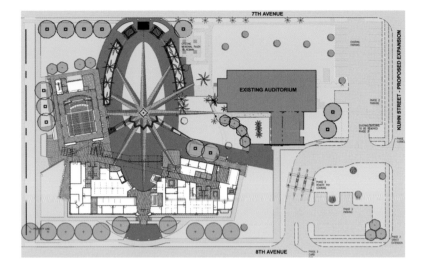

along the city's main axis through the structure's floor-to-parapet glass exterior. The porcelain and paver materials from the plaza will also appear in the lobby, furthering the indoor-outdoor relationship.

Going beyond Edinburg city officials' programmatic needs, TAG International helped expand their vision, leading to the creation of a community epicenter and civic destination predicated on a contemporary interpretation of the community's historical architectural language. ■ ■ ■ ■ ■ ■ ■ ■ ■ ■ ■

ABOVE: The project site is located on a major axis through the city that will connect the new city hall to the University of Texas–Pan American campus to the west and the Museum of South Texas History and the Hidalgo County Courthouse to the east.
Rendering by J. Crawley, courtesy of TAG International

RIGHT: The elliptical shape of the outdoor plaza continues through the main building lobby, connecting interior and exterior spaces visibly through a transparent glass wall.
Rendering by J. Crawley, courtesy of TAG International

FACING PAGE LEFT: The council chambers provide a multifunctional venue for public receptions, city meetings and cultural activities.
Rendering by J. Crawley, courtesy of TAG International

FACING PAGE RIGHT: This graphic representation shows the distribution of departments in the new Edinburg City Hall.
Rendering courtesy of TAG International

Frisco Career and Technical Education Center

SHW Group - Plano

■ ■ ■ ■ ■ ■ ■ ■ ■ ■ One of the fastest-growing school districts in Texas, Frisco Independent School District has garnered an outstanding reputation as an exemplary school system producing exceptional students. Seeking to provide its students with even greater educational opportunities, the district decided to offer its high school upperclassmen a rigorous curriculum that combines academics with hands-on learning. Frisco ISD worked intimately with SHW Group to program, plan and design Frisco Career and Technical Education Center, achieving a synergistic union that yielded a truly remarkable learning environment, which will establish a new paradigm for career- and technically based education.

ABOVE: The main entry façade expresses a sleek, contemporary character achieved through an assembly of metal panels and extensive glazing, which exhibits the center to the larger community.
Rendering by Randy Ehler and J.D. Toony, SHW Group

FACING PAGE: The exterior is defined by great transparency, representing a progressive aesthetic quality reflective of corporate-style buildings and the future of professional working environments.
Rendering by Randy Ehler and J.D. Toony, SHW Group

The new CTE Center is part of a larger master plan that will include the district's main administration building and potentially a future high school; the center is across the street from Collin County Community College, affording a valuable adjacency with an institution of higher education and availing college credit for many of the course offerings. Set on an undeveloped parcel in Frisco with mature trees and 27 feet of fall across the terrain, the architecture is an absolute response to the site and envisioned to be a true community focus. The structure steps down in several places to respond to the land's natural descent and is oriented to be prominently visible from any vantage on campus. As such, the exterior is one of great transparency, which lends itself to a progressive aesthetic quality associated with corporate-style facilities and the future of professional working environments.

Because the architectural fabric of Frisco—and its many school facilities—tends to be of a more traditional style, it was important that the Frisco CTE Center present a future-minded appearance, one that would instantly inform patrons they are entering a wholly unique environment. Thus the primary entrance façade conveys a slick, modern character achieved through an array of metal panels and extensive glazing, which showcases the center to the larger community. The entry atrium is a two-story volume with a large panel system of flat screens, instantly providing entrants with pertinent info; the main staircase abuts the glass exterior, exhibiting interior circulation and energy to passersby. While progressive in nature, the palette of metal, glass and terrazzo made from recycled glass and porcelain could exude an austere quality, so the sleek look is tempered by the use of exterior masonry for contrast as well as glue-laminated beams and a slatted wood ceiling. Structurally, clean lines and dramatic massing define the composition: Exposed cantilevers near the main entrance add great drama while large overhangs adorning the full-height glass make the roof systems feel like they are floating in space.

Programmatically, the center will be a truly singular offering. Unique components include a mock courtroom, forensics center, nursing facility, full-size high-definition television studio, a kennel for small animals and a corral for large animals for pre-veterinary students, a school retail store and a fully functioning restaurant. While many of these offerings are disparate in nature, the design team strove to establish interdisciplinary studies and find ways through technology, adjacencies and the large atrium space to connect them and encourage collaboration. Innovative and distinct, the Frisco Career and Technical Education Center has already drawn attention from around the state and even nationwide for its progressive model, which is sure to maintain and enhance Frisco ISD's superior reputation. ■ ■ ■ ■ ■ ■ ■ ■ ■

TOP RIGHT: A large panel system of flat screens in the two-story atrium instantly provides entrants with valuable information.
Rendering by Randy Ehler and J.D. Toony, SHW Group

BOTTOM RIGHT: The interior's sleek look is softened by the use of perimeter masonry as well as beams and a slatted wood ceiling.
Rendering by Randy Ehler and J.D. Toony, SHW Group

FACING PAGE: The main staircase fronts the glass exterior, displaying interior circulation and vitality to passersby.
Rendering by Randy Ehler and J.D. Toony, SHW Group

Hill Country Montessori

■■ ■■ ■ ■ ■ ■ ■ ■ ■ ■ ■ ■ ■ ■ ■ ■ ■ ■ ■ ■ ■

SHW Group - San Antonio

■ ■ ■ ■ ■ ■ ■ ■ ■ SHW Group's design for the Hill Country Montessori School is a quintessential example of how academia can not only influence an architectural design, but how the design of a holistic learning environment can be integrally connected to an academic approach and its corresponding curriculum. A response to the school's teaching method in which students are self-directed and teachers are there to guide and inform them along the path of self-discovery, SHW Group's design incorporates thoughtful sustainable design techniques that promote learning through architecture.

ABOVE: Natural and indigenous materials create the elegant design of the administration building, which acts as the main secure entry to the campus.
Rendering by Scott Deans

FACING PAGE: The classroom is designed to enhance the connectivity between the built environment and the natural surroundings to allow young minds to explore and learn in either setting.
Project Design Team: Christian Owens, Scott Deans, Jason Blanco, Daniel Perez, Joan Gallup and Greg Ferguson.
Rendering by Scott Deans

Located on a 10-acre parcel of land outside of Boerne, a genuine Hill Country ranch with live oaks, cedars and deer on site, the school will be delicately set among these natural elements to foster an intimate connection with nature while leaving minimal footprints. Small buildings house two classrooms each, and the buildings are designed so that the north- and south-facing walls are all glass while the east- and west-facing walls are solid stone to limit solar heat gain. Moreover, the expansive glass furthers the connection with the environment and the notion that the classroom is both interior and exterior.

The campus is a didactic tool itself, characterized by exposed building systems and valuable learning applications. The structure is all tongue-and-groove decking beneath a wood building, exhibiting the skeleton of the building and how it is held up. Exposed ductwork in classrooms demonstrates necessary heating and cooling functions. Outside, water is collected from the roof and travels through spigots into cisterns so students can actually see the water flow. The water flows from the cistern back into the irrigation collection system, so all irrigation is derived from the rainwater. Gardens are set around and watered from the cisterns, and the gardens include fruits and vegetables planted and maintained by students, representing another extension of the classroom.

A nature trail comprised of crushed gravel lines the site's perimeter and meanders through the native trees and vegetation, providing opportunities for children to traverse the terrain and learn about various

natural phenomena. SHW Group has encouraged administrators to expand upon the nature trail idea, incorporating information spots with descriptive text along the way, and even allow students to create their own unique pathways.

Wholly dedicated to designing learning environments that transcend buildings, SHW Group designed Hill Country Montessori as an academic campus that very much transcends mere walls and structural workings. By intimately connecting indoor and outdoor spaces, promoting classrooms without walls and championing environmental stewardship through the campus' sustainable design, SHW Group devised the ideal architectural solution for the students and curriculum of Hill Country Montessori. ■ ■ ■ ■ ■ ■ ■ ■ ■ ■ ■

ABOVE: Architecture is a learning tool to promote inclusivity, nature and awareness within academia as displayed through water collection, evaporative cooling sun-shades, community gardens and informal outdoor learning. Rendering by Scott Deans

FACING PAGE: Through sustainable practice, each building's minimal footprint is nestled between existing trees and natural systems, which are both major components to the Montessori curriculum. Rendering by Scott Deans

Legacy ER

■ ■

5Gstudio_collaborative

■ ■ ■ ■ ■ ■ ■ ■ ■ A departure from conventional healthcare design sensibilities, Legacy ER is a 6,175-square-foot hybrid emergency room and urgent care treatment facility north of Dallas in Frisco predicated on an environment for healing that emphasizes the power of tranquility. Designed for a trio of independent doctors who desired a progressive structure unlike typical, institutional treatment facilities, the architecture places great emphasis on improving the quality of healthcare spaces. 5Gstudio_collaborative approached the project with an eye toward hospitality, creating a lucid plan based around circulation and functionality with a spa-like interior quality, giving the doctors an award-winning custom design that is supportive of their practice and unparalleled in the healthcare realm.

ABOVE: Glowing transparent volumes at dusk emanate a tone of tranquility not found in typical healthcare facilities.
Rendering by 5Gstudio_collaborative

FACING PAGE: The distinctive, cantilevered roof canopy defines the main entry and bisects the entire building.
Project Design Team: Yen Ong, James Warton, Alesha Calvert, Warren Lieu and Hoang Dang.
Rendering by 5Gstudio_collaborative

The design employs an engaging assemblage of materials and spatial organization to create a soothing place of respite for emergency care. Two rectangular, fritted-glass volumes on the lower level—one for patients and one for resident doctors—are tucked underneath a light but continuous zinc-clad roof plane, which turns down at one end to provide enclosure for a landscape-screened patio area. Zinc was selected for its durability, sustainability and unique surface qualities; porcelain-fritted, low-E insulated glass was chosen as an energy-conscious glazing material that would allow natural light to pass while obscuring views to the interior and reducing the solar heat gain. The concrete floor and foundation were poured using integral color concrete, which was diamond-polished and left exposed throughout public areas. Serene outdoor space is afforded by the patio, which features a landscape-screen of fragrant jasmine ivy, cedar and the enchanting sounds of flowing water. A secondary plane beneath the roof canopy cantilevers out, serving as a welcoming beacon at the front entry, and bisects the entire building through the interior back to the nurse's station.

The simple diagram of the facility is one of clarity in circulation and function. Its main circulation corridor is organized to create an open environment, and light wells at the entrance to each treatment room introduce abundant daylight while articulating the primary lines of circulation. The door to each treatment

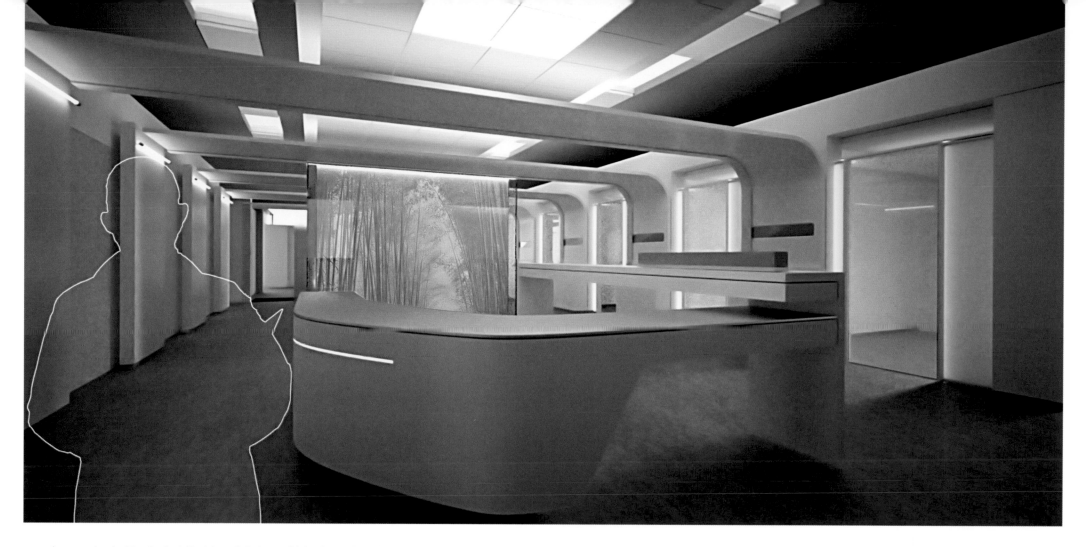

room is comprised of laminated, liquid crystal glass, which phases from transparent to opaque, giving patients privacy while enabling staff to ascertain the occupancy status of the room. Nurse's station, reception and laboratory areas form the backbone of the facility and are clad in a blend of translucent resin panels and etched glass layered in hues of green. The interior includes an array of green tones, along with vibrant, earthy montages and a spa-like ambience.

The design of Legacy ER incorporates eclectic materials ranging in levels of transparency, translucency and tactility to compose a spatial quality that is at once complex, soft and uplifting. Refined interior spaces and a modern exterior shell create a healthcare facility unlike others, and 5Gstudio_collaborative's design of Legacy ER was recognized nationally with a first-place award in a healthcare environment award competition from the Center for Health Design. ■ ■ ■ ■ ■ ■ ■ ■ ■ ■

ABOVE: The treatment corridors are rhythmically delineated with translucent, glazed openings bathed in natural daylight through skylight openings above.
Rendering by 5Gstudio_collaborative

FACING PAGE TOP: Landscaping and a green screen wall soften the simple, modern character of the building.
Rendering by 5Gstudio_collaborative

FACING PAGE BOTTOM: Transparent lobby space looks out toward the entry canopy, blurring the line between interior and exterior.
Rendering by 5Gstudio_collaborative

Legal Aid of NorthWest Texas

MULTATECH

For more than half a century a nonprofit group of dedicated private attorneys, bar and community leaders and law school professors currently known as Legal Aid of NorthWest Texas has worked to ensure equal justice for people living in poverty through the provision of high-quality legal representation. The organization's Fort Worth office, originally built in 1925 as a church, had received additions, renovations, partitions and other amendments over the years and become unsuitable for modern office usage. The laudable organization selected MULTATECH to design a new structure that will combine its Fort Worth and Arlington offices in a more efficient and functional building that evokes the old edifice and downtown Fort Worth's many design genres in a modern composition.

FACING PAGE: Prominently addressing the northwest corner of the intersection at Weatherford and Pecan streets, Legal Aid of NorthWest Texas deftly accommodates 20,000 square feet of space on a site that is less than one-half acre.
Project Design Team: Hong P. Chen, Benjamin A. Smith, Alan C. Sowerbrower and Dali Yang.
Rendering by MULTATECH

The existing building is set on an exceptionally stringent site, less than one-half acre, slightly northeast of downtown Fort Worth that would need to support 20,000 square feet of office space as well as parking. The design solution will maximize the available space by orienting the entry lobby to the corner of Weatherford Street and placing parking on the first floor behind it. More than just an efficient use of the available space, orienting the three-level circulation area toward the west and outfitting it with glass curtainwall will create a compelling entry sequence to patrons and also provide great visuals of downtown and its historic courthouse.

The material palette was extrapolated from the many periods of design evidenced throughout downtown Fort Worth, which includes both historic and modern buildings. Two tones of brick will define the first and second floors of the structure while the third floor will be skinned in aluminum composite panel with clear anodized aluminum frames and semi-reflective glazing. The front entry will be denoted by a glass canopy above and a cornered wing wall comprised of Roman travertine ornamented with subtle banding.

Paying homage to the old structure was a priority and the new structure will employ elements of the 1925-built building. The cornerstone from the original building was reclaimed and will be placed on the exterior corner of the building

LEFT: The structure's eclectic material palette is reflective of the Fort Worth urban fabric's array of design periods and vernaculars.
Rendering by MULTATECH

FACING PAGE LEFT: The front entry is denoted by a glass canopy, a cornered, travertine wing wall and a full-height curtainwall.
Rendering by MULTATECH

FACING PAGE RIGHT: Expansive glass in the interior lobby frames compelling views of Fort Worth; the city's historic downtown courthouse is a sterling visual from its nearby setting.
Rendering by MULTATECH

alongside a new plaque created from the back of the cornerstone—in days past the cornerstone was a solid triangle of stone, enabling the veneer to be separated from the rest of the mass for this purpose—that will give an indication of the history of the building. Salvaged bricks will be laid alongside new bricks to compose a paver at the entrance so that patrons will literally walk on the history of the building but step into a new design, which will enable Legal Aid of NorthWest Texas to grow and enhance its benevolent efforts into the future. ■ ■ ■ ■ ■ ■ ■ ■ ■ ■

The Mercantile

■ ■

Beeler Guest Owens Architects, Inc.

■ ■ ■ ■ ■ ■ ■ ■ ■ ■ Originally built in 1942, the Mercantile National Bank Building once stood as the tallest building in Texas and has been a compelling component of the Dallas skyline for decades. However, despite its prominent setting on Main Street in Dallas' central business district, as well as its striking mid-century modern architecture, the Mercantile has stood vacant since the early 1990s. Developer ForestCity Enterprises, in collaboration with architect of record Beeler Guest Owens Architects, is redeveloping the Mercantile complex, a full city block in the heart of the central business district, into a vital mixed-use development that will spur revitalization in downtown Dallas.

The 31-story Mercantile National Bank Building was the first structure built and centerpiece of what later became four distinct structures comprising the Mercantile National Bank Complex. Renowned for its Art Moderne styling from the Art Deco era, the famous edifice features a number of setbacks

FACING PAGE: Alongside the restored and redeveloped Mercantile Tower will be a new 16-story structure, which is designed to be a contemporary reinterpretation of the historic tower's mid-century modern aesthetic.
Project Design Team: Gary Pitts, Soussan Afsharfar, Cecilia Diaz, Love Pate, Denise Bates, Ed Hodges, Alex Adkins, Jeff Turner and Eric Antrim.
Rendering by DiMella Shaffer

that culminate in a stately clock tower, which is capped by a 115-foot-tall ornamental spire. While this remarkable structure was preserved and will be converted into 213 residential units over ground-floor retail, the other three structures were razed to make way for a new 16-story, 154-unit residential tower.

An essential requirement of adapting the historic edifice was that it be faithfully restored to its original 1942 design intent. Ample research and old black-and-white photos provided a guide for the design of the interiors. The kitchens, for example, are of a sleek and modern aesthetic, built more like a machine than a piece of furniture with exposed stainless steel and slick, glossy white cabinetry—much like kitchens of the 1950s known for their metal cabinets.

The new 16-story building is designed as the historic Mercantile's neighbor, a dynamic tower that creates a contemporary reinterpretation of the iconic mid-century modern images and motifs. Co-designed by Boston-based DiMella Shaffer, the new structure employs striking architectural elements such as a highly stylized roofline and a crown-like prow with an open steel frame that extends to the east, where a new park, Main Street Gardens, will provide a full city block of green space.

The two structures will be linked by a two-story building creating a single, secure entry point. This building will also feature a second-floor amenity level and views to the new exterior amenity deck. Three levels

of parking will be tucked underneath the amenity deck, which features an elaborate exterior plaza with grilling stations, fountains, waterfalls, a large pool and lush landscaping.

An exceptionally challenging and complex endeavor planned over many phases, the adaptation of the Mercantile National Bank Complex into a bold mixed-use development is key to the revitalization of the central business district and will undoubtedly be a catalyst for urban renewal in this vital sector of downtown Dallas. ■ ■ ■ ■ ■ ■ ■ ■ ■ ■

ABOVE LEFT: The second-floor amenity level will feature an exterior deck replete with a large pool, waterfalls, barbecue grills and lush landscaping.
Rendering by MESA

ABOVE RIGHT: A grand architectural endeavor of immense complexity, The Mercantile will comprise a full city block in Dallas' central business district and help revitalize a vital urban area.
Rendering by DiMella Shaffer and MESA

FACING PAGE LEFT: Varying ceiling heights are reflected in the corridor's carpet, lending interest to an essential artery of circulation.
Rendering by DiMella Shaffer

FACING PAGE RIGHT: A single entry point will provide access to both buildings, affording valuable security to residents and patrons.
Rendering by DiMella Shaffer

Needville High School

SHW Group - Houston

When school district officials from Needville ISD met with architects from SHW Group to discuss the design of the forthcoming Needville High School, the desire emerged for a school rooted in the local context that defines the area's agricultural nature. Conceived as an assembly of smaller structures integrally connected with the landscape, the design for this learning environment avoids the conventional brick-box style of most schools, evoking the agrarian traditions found throughout Needville.

From Main Street to the rural countryside, SHW Group explored Needville in search of its architectural character by studying, documenting and photographing the different elements that make up its community. From this expedition the design team took away a sense of ingenuity from the

FACING PAGE: The design of Needville High School capitalizes on the voluminous landscape through a series of structures assembled as a collage of buildings on a farmstead.
Project Design Team: Mark Lam, Tracy Eich, Chris Hinton, Stuart Williams and Luis Ayala.
Rendering by SHW Group

structures, noting the emphasis on function over aesthetics that is prevalent in rural life. This notion inspired Needville's design—a machine aesthetic with an agrarian theme.

As with each school designed by SHW Group, the academic program that will take place within the structure was priority number one. Needville's design will allow the student body to be organized around grade-level, small learning communities with the flexibility to reorganize by academic departments.

The architectural response takes advantage of the immense landscape on the 250-acre tract of agricultural land via a series of buildings assembled like a collage of buildings on a farmstead. Each building represents a different programmatic piece of the school's educational components. At the heart of the facility is a centrally located student gathering space designed as a silo feature. As the conduit between the main street corridor and the two academic wings that flank the silo, this gathering space serves as the focal point for student interaction and circulation from one class to the next, providing students with a sense of order. The two academic wings, which house the small learning communities, are organized around a courtyard that frames the view to the science building, a distinctive feature of the campus with exhaust hoods and a

TOP LEFT: The library is identified from both the exterior and interior by a field wall of stacked stone, which is independent of the building structure.
Rendering by SHW Group

BOTTOM LEFT: Curved auditorium walls, corrugated metal panels and natural light frame the auditorium stage, making it and the event taking place the focal point.
Rendering by SHW Group

FACING PAGE LEFT: The gymnasium is flooded with natural light and highlighted by exposed steel trusses while the weight room on the second floor overlooks the basketball courts.
Rendering by SHW Group

FACING PAGE RIGHT: The dining room is reminiscent of a pavilion with exposed trusses, a cupola and extensive areas of glass that allow natural light to fill the space.
Rendering by SHW Group

green screen in the form of latticework and vines on the west façade. The courtyard will provide students an outdoor learning lab to conduct experiments and research.

Throughout the building students will be surrounded by ample glass that frames the landscape, serving to acknowledge the land's integral role within the community. This transparency is also carried throughout the interior of the school. The library, dining area, theater and competition gymnasium have extensive

areas of glass so as students make their way down the main street corridor they may see the interesting activities or events underway.

A partner of Needville ISD for two decades, SHW Group created a design for Needville High School that maintains the independence of this small community and will provide students with an inspirational learning environment reflective of their community's connection to the land. ■ ■ ■ ■ ■ ■ ■ ■ ■ ■ ■

Trinity Uptown

● ■

Gideon Toal

■ ■ ■ ■ ■ ■ ■ ■ ■ In recent years there has been a nationwide movement to reconnect urban citizens and downtown districts with their respective waterfronts. What started out as a plan to improve Trinity River flood control in Fort Worth blossomed into a comprehensive effort to attract residents to live in the central core of the city in a walkable, sustainable development that will consolidate growth around downtown. As the lead consultant on a substantial and skilled team of collaborators that includes the U.S. Army Corps of Engineers, Bing Thom Architects and CDM, Gideon Toal has provided services on Trinity Uptown in the areas of planning, public information gathering, consensus building, workshops, design, phasing, implementation and funding strategies. Gideon Toal played a pivotal role in this ambitious mixed-use development that will conserve and respect the history of the Trinity while adding significant density and vitality to an 800-acre area north of downtown Fort Worth.

ABOVE: The east side of the proposed bypass channel is envisioned as a hard edge with upper- and lower-level pedestrian walkways. The west or soft edge of the bypass channel will be designed as a park-like natural setting with trails that connect to the length of the greenbelt.
Rendering by Kevin Wilson, courtesy of Trinity River Vision Authority

FACING PAGE: Trinity Uptown will provide improved flood control and reconnect urban Fort Worth with the Trinity River.
Rendering by Kevin Wilson, courtesy of Trinity River Vision Authority

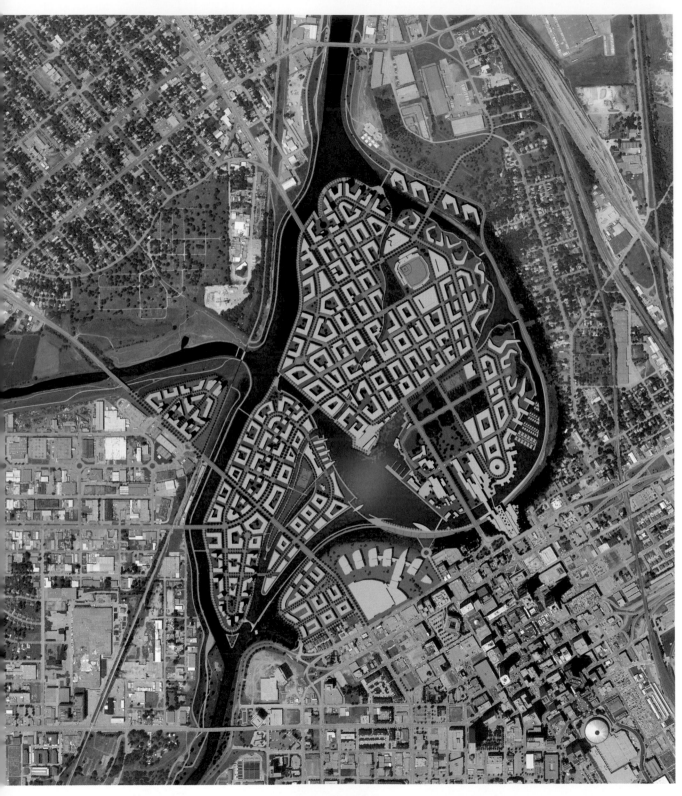

Improved flood control and a constant water level will be attained by creating a stormwater bypass around the central urban area thanks to dams. In the event of heavy rainfall, floodgates will close and the bypass channel will route floodwater around this area, which allows engineers to eliminate existing levees and build down to the water's edge. An overriding objective is to reconnect urban Fort Worth with the Trinity River and encourage activity on the water and along waterfront areas. In addition to eliminating the existing levees, 12 miles of accessible waterfront trails and promenades will be created. Two 50-foot-wide east-west flowing canals will create compelling residential environments, and all water bodies will be navigable by kayaks, canoes and rowboats; small water taxis will operate on the main water bodies to link various destinations.

Much of Trinity Uptown's activity will be staged around a compelling urban lake, which will provide a wealth of uses and be a focal point of the development. Approximately 35 percent of the site will be devoted to public open space, including public plazas and parks with their own distinctive identities that correspond to one of four distinct neighborhoods. The site's strategic location in the center of Fort Worth between downtown, the cultural district and the near northside and Stockyards districts presents a valuable opportunity to integrate housing into the central city; the plan proposes eventually adding 10,000 new households in mixed-use neighborhoods. Each neighborhood will be distinctive in character, supported by its own schools, commercial, retail and institutional buildings; the southeast neighborhood will be closely associated with a dynamic new Tarrant County College downtown campus—which will be built on both sides of and span the river.

Incorporating watershed management and environmental restoration strategies for a dynamic, sustainable urban environment, the Trinity Uptown plan will create a resurgence in Fort Worth's central core by adding 12 million square feet of mixed-use, primarily residential, development that will conserve and respect the rich history of the confluence of the Trinity River, the birthplace of Fort Worth and Tarrant County. ■ ■ ■ ■ ■ ■ ■ ■ ■

TOP RIGHT: An entertainment and cultural hub of activity thrives around the historic TXU power plant on the proposed urban lake.
Rendering by Kevin Wilson, courtesy of Trinity River Vision Authority

BOTTOM RIGHT: The north canal will provide direct waterfront access for residents and visitors alike, bringing pedestrians back to the river's edge.
Rendering by Kevin Wilson, courtesy of Trinity River Vision Authority

FACING PAGE: An aerial perspective of the master plan with the proposed bypass channel and urban lake illustrates the project's extensive scope.
Rendering by Kevin Wilson, courtesy of Trinity River Vision Authority

Vitruvian Park

Kevin Sloan Studio

The town of Addison, a northern Dallas suburb, is known as a forward-thinking community with a thoughtful and attentive government and numerous entertainment options. Thus it makes sense that Addison will be home to Vitruvian Park—a distinctive, sustainable urban development in which outdoor spaces are celebrated and integrally intertwined with daily life, providing residents a place that is truly a framework for living. An ambitious urban infill project encompassing five phases over 16 years, Vitruvian Park is a harbinger of responsible urban development—a live, work and play environment designed on an appealing human scale for active urban dwellers.

Named after Vitruvius, the ancient Roman architect whose great treatise on architecture and humanism would later inspire Leonardo di Vinci to produce his drawing, *Vitruvian Man*, the nearly 100-acre development is a place designed for the human being first. Project developer UDR is spearheading this

FACING PAGE: As one of four neighborhood centers, this park is an offering to nature, featuring cypress-covered islands and spring-fed waters that emerge from a grotto fountain depicted in the background.
Project Design Team: Mark Culwell, Tom Lamberth, Kevin Sloan and Sarah Mundy.
Rendering by Michael McCann, Kevin Sloan Studio

bold endeavor and enlisted Kevin Sloan Studio as the project's master planner and urban designer—Kevin is determining the form of the community, the layout of spaces and building heights and developing a pattern book to establish an architectural code of cohesion as the project unfolds in phases. Kevin Sloan Studio is also serving as landscape architect, designing in detail the parks, streetscapes and the public spaces between buildings.

Vitruvian Park's urban fabric will feature a network of streets, parks and squares that are organized around four distinct neighborhood centers that will establish identity for the housing in their immediate environs. A key feature distinguishing the community from other New Urbanist developments is the integration of an existing spring-fed watercourse, a finger of Farmers Branch Creek, which will be expanded and reconfigured into a broad surface pond with cypress-planted islands that are usable for leisure. The development is designed in accordance with human dimensions with walkable, tree-lined streets that are scaled to walking distances throughout, and spaces within buildings are thought of as deliberately proportioned rooms.

The centerpiece of the many parks and planned outdoor spaces will be a 12-acre parcel of gently sloping lawn surfaces built around a meandering spring-fed creek; the park will connect to area bicycle and jogging trails as well as all four neighborhood centers. The channel encircling the park will feature a

series of boat-shaped islands planted with cypress trees and dawn redwoods, giving the park a larger presence and the semblance of looking through landscaped screens. In addition to grade changes and a number of compelling bridges—such as a suspension bridge with an impressive steel arch and some that will traverse the pond some 25 feet over the water—the park includes a remarkable grotto fountain, which will connect beautiful Vitruvian Parkway to a lower-level pool with a dramatic water drop.

Mindful of the ancient principles of Vitruvius, Vitruvian Park will provide urbanites with a wonderful and splendid array of experiences through a mélange of engaging, usable exterior spaces in a sustainable development—a place that fosters living—establishing a new paradigm locally for responsible urban development. ■ ■ ■ ■ ■ ■ ■ ■ ■ ■

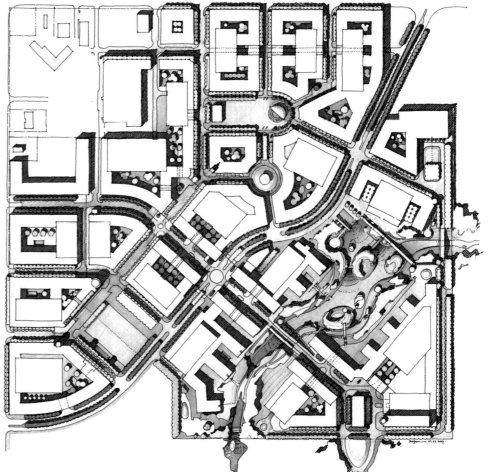

ABOVE: Vitruvian Park is a place of contrasts and surprises in urban space, as seen in the varying scale of the phase one buildings designed by WDG Architecture.
Rendering courtesy of WDG Architecture

RIGHT: An existing street diagonal is retained as Vitruvian Park Boulevard, which acts as an urban seam between the residential densities, mixed uses and open-space network of the plan.
Rendering by Kevin Sloan, Kevin Sloan Studio

FACING PAGE: Vitruvian Park's dense fabric and mixed-use network of public parks and spaces provide urbanites with a host of opportunities in a naturalistic setting.
Rendering by Michael McCann, Kevin Sloan Studio

Woodlands Grill at Watters Creek

Techcon Dallas, Inc.

■ ■ ■ ■ ■ ■ ■ ■ ■ ■ Providing a modern interpretation of classic American cuisine, Woodlands Grill is an exciting restaurant franchise in which Frank Lloyd Wright-inspired architecture presents a compelling contemporary backdrop ideally suited for enjoying innovative interpretations of American fare. As the fourth location of this unique restaurant offering, Woodlands Grill at Watters Creek, located in the heart of a prestigious mixed-use development in Allen, will bring an inviting new upscale dining option to north Texas.

Designed by Bruce Russo of Techcon Dallas, Woodlands Grill is inspired by the extraordinary designs of Frank Lloyd Wright—particularly by Wright's magnum opus, Fallingwater, but also by his Prairie School vernacular and other captivating designs—and Wrightian influences are evidenced in abundant natural stone, rich hardwoods and clean contemporary lines. Much as Wright's designs so often deftly employed horizontal motifs, Woodlands Grill conveys

FACING PAGE: Stucco awnings and stone columns surround the entryway of Woodlands Grill, adding an earthy feel and a strong linear appearance.
Project Design Team: Bruce Russo, Joe Russo, Laura Fate and Victor Badillo.
Rendering by CG Rendering

a grand sense of the horizontal through ubiquitous horizontal banding and an array of levels, which ever so subtly create an appropriate human scale that is wholly engaging to patrons. This inviting aura is further conveyed through the varying planes of the ceiling topography—for example, eight-foot-tall ceilings in booths give way to 12-foot-tall ceilings just outside, creating interest and spaces of intimacy and repose.

Abundant glass is a defining feature that, along with a prevalence of stone on both the exterior and interior, blurs the line between inside and outside and creates continuity throughout the space. Moreover, stately stone used on the exterior comprises the front of the bar and a remarkable stone fireplace behind; a compelling water feature at the bar displays water cascading down glass between sculpture, which in many ways conveys the feeling of the creek's running water at Fallingwater.

A singular restaurant concept in which the architecture is equally if not more compelling than the menu, Woodlands Grill at Watters Creek utilizes Wright's trademark horizontal flair and subtle but engaging details as interpreted by Techcon Dallas to create the perfect setting for enjoying contemporary culinary creations that, much like Wright himself, are uniquely American. ■ ■ ■ ■ ■ ■ ■ ■ ■ ■ ■

TOP RIGHT: Wood paneling creates a dramatic accent on feature walls, which are arrayed with accessories to add a touch of home. Period carvings adorn the booth walls, adding subtle elegance.
Rendering by CG Rendering

BOTTOM RIGHT: The furniture at Woodlands, made of rich cherry hardwood, adds to the harmonious balance of new design with a classical sense of style.
Rendering by CG Rendering

FACING PAGE LEFT: The grand stone fireplace flanked by stylized, floating wood shelves adds warmth and style to the bar, making it the perfect place to relax.
Rendering by CG Rendering

FACING PAGE RIGHT: The suspended ceiling details and use of fine wood materials convey the rich character seen throughout Wright's designs.
Rendering by CG Rendering

CITY BY DESIGN TEXAS

TEXAS TEAM
ASSOCIATE PUBLISHER: Karla Setser
GRAPHIC DESIGNER: Ashley Rodges
EDITOR: Ryan Parr
PRODUCTION COORDINATOR: Laura Greenwood

HEADQUARTERS TEAM
PUBLISHER: Brian G. Carabet
PUBLISHER: John A. Shand
EXECUTIVE PUBLISHER: Phil Reavis
DIRECTOR OF DEVELOPMENT & DESIGN: Beth Benton Buckley
DIRECTOR OF BOOK MARKETING & DISTRIBUTION: Julia Hoover
PUBLICATION MANAGER: Lauren B. Castelli
SENIOR GRAPHIC DESIGNER: Emily A. Kattan
GRAPHIC DESIGNER: Jonathan Fehr
EDITORIAL DEVELOPMENT SPECIALIST: Elizabeth Gionta
MANAGING EDITOR: Rosalie Z. Wilson
EDITOR: Katrina Autem
EDITOR: Amanda Bray
EDITOR: Anita M. Kasmar
EDITOR: Daniel Reid
MANAGING PRODUCTION COORDINATOR: Kristy Randall
PRODUCTION COORDINATOR: Amanda Johnson
PRODUCTION COORDINATOR: Drea Williams
TRAFFIC COORDINATOR: Meghan Anderson
ADMINISTRATIVE MANAGER: Carol Kendall
ADMINISTRATIVE ASSISTANT: Beverly Smith
CLIENT SUPPORT COORDINATOR: Amanda Mathers
CLIENT SUPPORT ASSISTANT: Aimee Beresford

PANACHE PARTNERS, LLC
CORPORATE HEADQUARTERS
1424 Gables Court
Plano, TX 75075
469.246.6060
www.panache.com

Trinity Uptown, Gideon Toal, page 320
Rendering by Kevin Wilson, courtesy of Trinity River Vision Authority

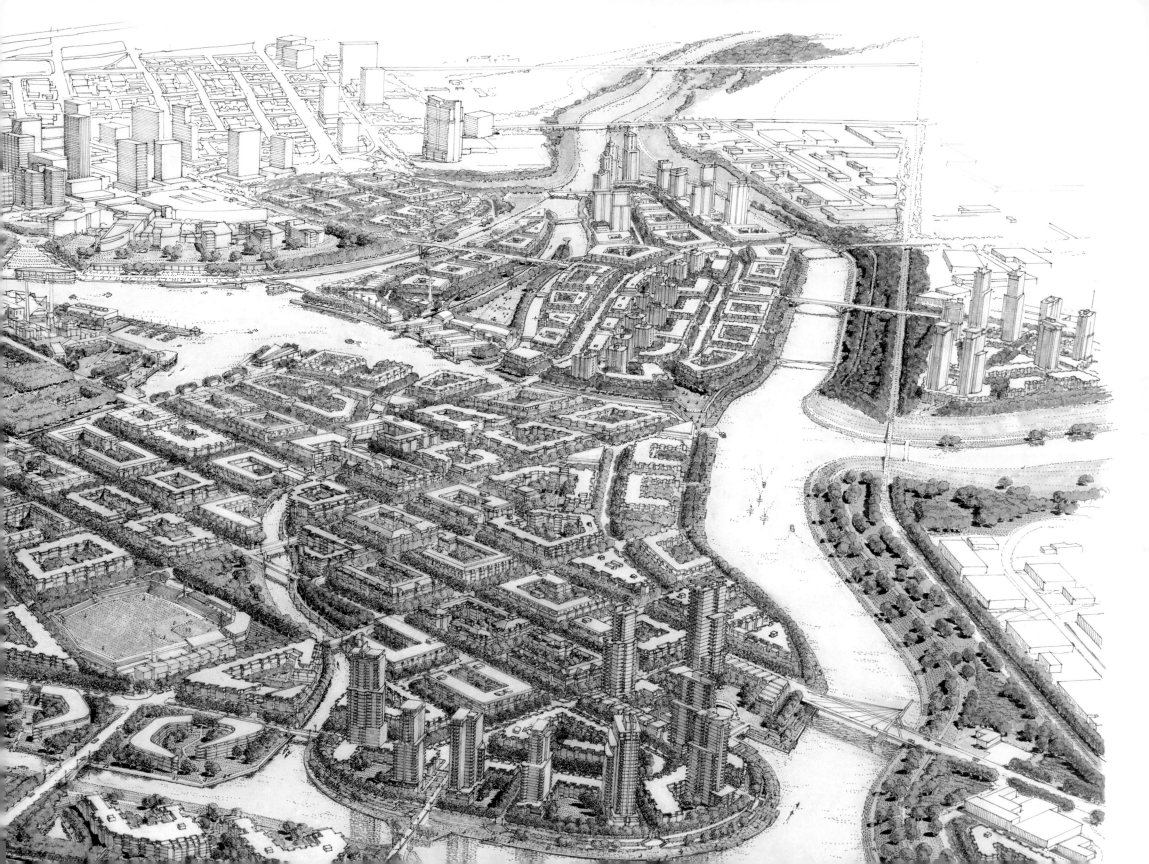

INDEX

THE PANACHE COLLECTION

CREATING SPECTACULAR PUBLICATIONS FOR DISCERNING READERS

Dream Homes Series
An Exclusive Showcase of the Finest Architects, Designers and Builders

Carolinas
Chicago
Coastal California
Colorado
Deserts
Florida
Georgia
Los Angeles
Metro New York
Michigan
Minnesota
New England
New Jersey

Northern California
Ohio & Pennsylvania
Pacific Northwest
Philadelphia
South Florida
Southwest
Tennessee
Texas
Washington, D.C.

Perspectives on Design Series
Design Philosophies Expressed by Leading Professionals

Carolinas
Chicago
Colorado
Florida
Georgia
Minnesota
New England

Pacific Northwest
San Francisco
Southwest
Texas

Spectacular Wineries Series
A Captivating Tour of Established, Estate and Boutique Wineries

California Central Coast
Napa Valley
New York
Sonoma

Spectacular Homes Series
An Exclusive Showcase of the Finest Interior Designers

California
Carolinas
Chicago
Colorado
Florida
Georgia
Heartland
London
Michigan
Minnesota
New England
New York
Ohio & Pennsylvania

Pacific Northwest
Philadelphia
South Florida
Southwest
Tennessee
Texas
Toronto
Washington, D.C.
Western Canada

City by Design Series
An Architectural Perspective

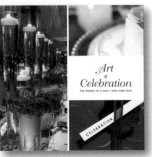

Atlanta
Charlotte
Chicago
Dallas
Denver
Orlando
Phoenix
San Francisco
Texas

Art of Celebration Series
The Making of a Gala

Florida Style
New York Style
Washington, D.C. Style

Specialty Titles

Distinguished Inns of North America
Extraordinary Homes California
London Homes

London Architects
Spectacular Golf of Colorado
Spectacular Golf of Texas

Spectacular Hotels
Spectacular Restaurants of Texas
Visions of Design

Panache Partners, LLC   1424 Gables Court   Plano, Texas 75075   469.246.6060   www.panache.com